CHINA BLUES

819   Donnell, David, 1939-
.154   China blues : poems and stories / David Donnell. --
Donne   Toronto : McClelland & Stewart, c1992.
            142 p.

        06314236   ISBN:0771028431 (pbk.)

        I. Title

6009   92MAY25   06/wi   1-00581818

Also by David Donnell

CHINA BLUES

POEMS AND STORIES

David Donnell

M&S

Canadian Cataloguing in Publication Data

Donnell, David, 1939–
China blues

Poems.
ISBN 0-7710-2843-1

1. Toronto (Ont.) – Poetry. I. Title.

PS8557.O55C5 1992   C811'.54   C92-093071-9
PR9199.3.D65C5 1992

The publisher makes grateful acknowledgement to the Ontario
Arts Council for its financial assistance.

Set in Sabon by The Typeworks, Vancouver
Printed and bound in Canada on acid-free paper

McClelland & Stewart Inc.
The Canadian Publishers
481 University Ave.
Toronto, Ontario M5G 2E9

For Robert Markle

Great spirit, great painter,
b. 1936—d. 1990

"A paper published in *Science* in November, 1987—and signed by enough geologists to make a quorum at the Rose Bowl—offers evidence that the San Andreas has folded its flanking country, much as a moving boat crossing calm waters will send off lateral waves."

> —JOHN MCPHEE, *Los Angeles Against the Mountains*

"I don't like rock music; I don't know why I'm in it. I just want to destroy everything."

> —JOHN LYDDON, The Sex Pistols, lead singer on "Dancing" and "God Save the Queen"

"One of Traylor's pictures shows a huge, mastiff-like dog towering above a small white man who holds his leash. But the leash is slack, the dog is calm, and the idea of the man controlling the dog absurd. The two proceed as companions."

> —PHIL PATTON, writing on 1940s black folk artist Bill Traylor, *Esquire*, September 1991

AUTHOR'S NOTE

My title comes from an interest in China and Chinese history, Delta blues, the road-blocks that were set up outside the Chinese consulate on St. George St. in Toronto in 1989, which I pass on my midday walks, traffic barricades piled high with flowers at that time for several days after Tienanmen Square; a number of expressions such as China Hand, All the tea in . . ., etc.; and last, but not least, Greg Couillard's excellent—and now in other hands—Toronto restaurant called China Blues. I think China Blues is a melancholy and a joyful book, and the title seems to me, at least, to be apt.

DAVID DONNELL
Toronto, Fall '91

Contents

MARCEL PROUST

Dope isn't like photographs or album covers, or Ward's Island photographs of old girlfriends, or a first printing of Mark Strand's *An Elegy For My Father,* or Jack Nicholson driving north in that vintage film, *Five Easy Pieces,* after giving up on Susan Anspach. Now there's a cool actress you don't see very much anymore. So, doodly: Woodle. I'm going to be infantile this afternoon, and then I'm going to be adult this evening because we're having people for dinner. Katharine Ross was brilliant in *Butch Cassidy & The Sundance Kid.* Let me confess something of very little importance, I've never read beyond the first few pages of that long book by Marcel Proust, and thinking of all the different things I have to do, I doubt very much if I ever will — especially if this sunny afternoon becomes any bluer.

THOSE KLEIN UNDERWEAR MEN

for Angela Morrow

        Gay women love men's bodies. And she said,
"No, they don't,
             that's ridiculous." So I said, lazily,
"Well, okay, not fat men's bodies, not guys with thick fur
down the backs of their necks,
not square-faced guys in rumpled suits. But what about
tall clean well-built guys with a clean shave
a nice tan & a snow white singlet?" She said, "Well,
that does sound a little more attractive."
                              And it's true,
of course it's true. At parties sometimes you'll see
a woman leaning all over some comfortable easy-going
well-built young guy, baby smooth shave
nice cornflower blue eyes, a tan
&, of course that white singlet. There's some
shoulder stroking,
& naturally they're both laughing. "O wipe your hand,"
he says in a really funky voice,
sloppy jeans but the singlet is really an S-curve
under the belt,
"I'm all sweaty," he says, & laughs at it. She strokes
him anyway, flashing her lipsticked mouth. She can't get
enough of it, because his body's so nice to touch. She
just doesn't want to have intercourse,
                        that's all;
&, thinking about it, why should she? Intercourse

should probably be reserved for really intimate
situations,
                occasions that take place in a
comfortable structure of intimacy. What she would
really like to do most with this guy
is just roll around on a huge white bed
preferably if he would stay on one elbow
part of the time,
                that would be nice, she thinks
just roll around heaven all day.

MANGOES

     East of Eden
             with its myth of the boy moving
away from the family was written for me.
They gave me a copy for my birthday when I was 11. There
    were
other factors. There were other novels.
There was always a sense of blue infinity
simpler & more marvellous than headmasters at UTS
could have dreamed of slumped
(Philosophers get tired their heads swollen like Grade A eggs)
Protestant & red-faced in western Ontario white pine chairs
unable to define infinity
although we found it easy to live. And by the time I was 20,
or 23½, or 24,
my favourite streets were Gloucester, Dundonald, Isabella.
                                            The
east of the city. There was always an abundance of chicken pot
pies & good cold beer.
                   There was no gaga social pressure
or rigid white pine chairs in those rundown Victorian
2nd floors I lived in on Church,
                    cross streets:
Dundonald, Gloucester, Isabella,
                   to do anything
except enjoy myself.
             I was happy. I read a lot
& drank quite a bit
           but I wasn't comfortable.

And when I came back
to what people generously refer to
as the liberal arts,
                    Saturday Night
& *Toronto Life,* I was testy. Other people
were variously snotty or generous.
                              I was testy
& sometimes it would affect my body,
                                   tension,
muscle spasm,
                    seizure of light
the jellyfish of light rising up in my mind
like a West African beach trophy. "Just cloud patterns,"
a friend of mine said to me, "go with it, and see where
it goes." Okay. I went.

                    These days I want to work all morning
until I'm tired,
                    and then sit in my blue dojo pants
like somebody back from a holiday in Tibet and watch the
        traffic
go past.
            The weather looks good for the next few years.
I miss Church Street
                        (and the way it empties east of Yonge
south through the city and into the Lake) sometimes
                                                    but
in a fairly abstract way. Postcards. The things
I love most are like pale green fruit, papayas, sour-sop, pale
        green
mangoes.

Touch them to my face in the warm Toronto sun, and
say,
thank you. That was nice. The roast lamb was fantastic. The
rosemary was sweet & bitter & my whole mouth feels fresh
again.

CHINA BLUES

China Blues is a song that Miles Davis never got around to writing,
& Oscar Peterson hasn't written yet.   >   John A. Macdonald,
Yukio Mishima, Billie Holliday. People whose names will be writ-
ten on the subway walls as far south as Massachusetts, where you
can garden as late as September, or as far west as Great Slave Lake –
where the big-eyed Loons sing cold & clear.   >   You might think of
John Lone in Bertolucci's film *The Last Emperor,* the scene at the
afternoon party where he sings a slow 30s Gershwin song with
English vowels & just a trace of Chinese accent.

   Or Molly Johnson singing "Cry Me A River" at a small club on
Queen Street West late at night before we walk up to Massimo's on
College Street & get a large *primavera* from the young Thai kid on
the front counter.   >   Or those long sad notes on the Chinese cello I
heard from a young Chinese student, shaven head, good musician,
from Burma, what was Burma, in the subway at University &
Queen.   >   Isn't this what Bessie Smith talked about when she first
started to record? She had a stars&stripes earring in her left ear, &
she said, I'll slow your boat down, & I'll send us both to China.   >
Of course it's a metaphor. But it does make you think of Mrs. Bed-
ford Stuyvestant-Fish, & Ben Johnson, the fastest man in the world,
& of Walker Evans, & of Li Po, who wrote such beautiful poems
about early morning air & light on the Niagara escarpment. If you
look north on a clear day you can see as far as Thunder Bay.

AVA

It's funny, though, that I should
think of Ava tonight. How she used to walk through hotel
lobbies in dark mink & heels
with nothing underneath.
Apparently she had hearts embroidered on her underwear.
Those hearts & lime green shoes & the black floor
& walls of this club shine up through the soft
indirect lighting that Billie
seems to be singing about while she gives Cole Porter
a nudge in the short ribs. Billie was always friendly,
whatever group she was working with she set up a good
rapport. I'm hot these days, the writing is good,
we've got Ontario garden peas in the stores,
Mexican garden peas, & California garden peas. The summer
weather rolls in & there don't seem to be no reason
why it should end. All I really want
from the world at this exact moment, before we leave
& I go home to sleep with M with one leg sprawled
over her ankle is some cappuccino
&,
        if I can get the waitress over here,
another play of that tape which begins
with an atypical cut of Joan Armatrading singing, "You
Give Me Fever." You do. Yes you do.

TOBACCO HEAVEN

for Russell Smith

                    The Surgeon General has told us firmly,
in that clipped voice,
                              pushing out his impressive beard,
he looks almost like a Mennonite
except that Mennonites are not so articulate
& they do not have a Yale accent,
                                        we must throw our cigarettes
away, & we must put on condoms.
                                        So here we are, okay,
world of wonders?
                        standing naked
although Paul has a pair of running shoes
& Neil is wearing red&yellow Argyle socks,
                                        out in front of
Mrs. Smith's Cocktail Party, across from The Bovine Sex Club
on Queen Street West,
                        it is a Tuesday afternoon
& it is sunny, the temperature is about 23°
& the barometer must be at least 102.5. We have thrown
our cigarettes away, hurled them, various garbage cans
over the last month, & we are restless. We are all wearing
condoms; put on a condom soft & walk around – it looks
amusing, I think, & affectionate; & we have all sorts
of different colours: charcoal grey, noir, natural, raspberry,
cerise, chromium blue, butter yellow, you name it, the boys
have gotten dressed before dinner.

We are not the hottest
kids to ever come out of the U of T graduate school,
but we are not
oafs, we are open minds. Frank comes out of the restaurant
& he says, "I can't stand it. I'm going to open up a Walter
Raleigh," & he lights up a rich Virginia cigarette, inhales
& blows the smoke out gracefully. He is tall with a shock
of flaming red hair & an angular body.
Elizabeth I, she
had flaming red hair also, she was crazy, sometimes,
Frank is not crazy, & sometimes they had to chain
her to the bed. Then Alvin comes out & sniffs the air
& winks one blue eye. "Wonder when," he says,
"they will get around to issuing us those neat handkerchief
& elastic strap face-masks you see guys wearing in Tokyo?"

We all laugh, standing with our hands in our pockets,
        sic,
leaning against the warm tiles & glass of the front wall
with our hands behind our heads,
                        resting on our hips,
or on each other's shoulders. We are waiting to see
what new car designs & Mies van der Rohe buildings
the 90s will bring. "Bet you some crab & 2 Double Diamonds
that the Jays win a pennant this year." "I'll bet *you*,"
he says, "a double crab & 2 Double Diamonds
that Jay McInerney never brings out his next book."
We all laugh, standing around in the sunshine.
We are waiting for the 90s.

Most newspaper articles are not as clear as Thomas Wolfe or Margaret Laurence talking about how you don't know who you are until you go away, and stop and look back, and see the stone angel in the town you come from – the house where you lived, the smell of the grass, tar on the gravel driveway. The large front windows are lit up, circa 5:30, it must be around 1950; your mother walks from the car up the front steps with a large brown paper bag of groceries and closes the large white front door with its 3 window panes behind her. A flash of gold wedding band, and she doesn't look back over her shoulder. > I feel that I have lost a large chunk of time. Ontario time I guess, the 40 years or so before I was even born. It has fallen out of my pocket like a grey rock with patches of inside colour. > I think Laurence is very good but she focuses too much on the family as a social unit; Thomas Wolfe is a truly great writer, the unfolding of a giant camera, I'm not saying this because he was tall, good-looking, or because he wrote on top of a fridge at one point. > Open *Look Homeward, Angel* at almost any page and you will see what I mean. The stone comes back into my pocket. > How can we talk about what Ontario was like 40 years ago without talking about the general mood of idealism in America as a whole at that time? > Why do we persist in the belief that Marilyn French OR Bret Easton Ellis are talking about anything of any significance? > I think it's amazing that so few people read Thomas Wolfe these days. I think it's amazing that so few people read Mary McCarthy and Edmund Wilson. These days.

We're in late spring or early summer now
in Alliston. Last night
it began getting dark around 8:30.
I have been a little melancholy for the last week,
& Alliston has been a relief.
                              Love's like that.
I had eaten supper, some fish & a mixed stir-fry of bell
peppers, & I began to think about how beautiful
the dark is.

                    So I went outside & stood with my back
against the wall of the house
                              & let my eyes play over
the dark backyard
smudged poplars & elms, soft dark late-night hawks
& distant voices,
                    to watch the darkness doing nothing
except being itself.
                              But after a while
I began to feel that our little affair was foolish;
in fact I began to feel our affair, your underwear,
your reddish golden hair,
                              can I be gender conscious,
thank you, *grazie,* your perfect sweet-tipped pair,
wash slowly out of my *kopf.* It's hard to be serious
about an imagined resentment

while you're staring at a whole Milky Way full of
stars.

       Probably a couple of rabbits down at the end
of the garden
          don't think I noticed them
squinting a bit to see the colour of
yellow zinnias
or the shiny bounce of small light
on a steel trowel left out from the afternoon.
No light from my friend Duck Moon. Should be a
fine dark yellow fingernail paring in another
week or so.
       And then I will write about you
as a woman I meet on a fall day in a train station,
in Zurich, or in Kansas going all the way south
to Texas to see your aunt.
          You Chinese goldfish,
you sexy bitch, full of planning your first child
with your black tie stockbroker husband,
you English crumpet, look at me in the dark,
I'm blushing like an Italian schoolboy
with fistfuls of change who can't find his handkerchief
for the sake of looking.

       I have been thinking about Madonna
on this blue April morning,
about how pretty she is, & how good she is
at faking defiance.
              I like the Madonna video
called "Justify
          My Love." I think Gaultier designed
the cone-nippled bra she wears
with a clear & full perfection, but nobody wrote
a Persian Gulf video for her to bop to.
                  Although
all she ever does is tilt her head back
& grab her crotch.
             But when she
does that
         she does me, what can I say? there is something
extraordinarily beautiful about her eyes, blue
                         blue
blue, like Neil
Young singing " . . . there is a town in north Ontari io."
Don't mistake me.
            I don't want to pick on Madonna.
She's terrific. She flaunts a form
of fundamental sexuality with a beautiful arrogance.
But it's a mistake
         to assume she's defiant. We're
just talking about having a good time. What
does she defy?
         And as for singing

let's tell the whole dangerous truth.
She hasn't got a good voice. Madonna can't sing for beans.

●

There's Norman Schwarzkopf across the street
short hair raw slab face dark glasses,
big 60 lb. beer gut
hanging over his twill pants. He has a short-sleeved
Hawaiian sport shirt
on; and is signing autographs
as he moves through a crowd of people in Boston,
I think;
or perhaps it's Philadelphia. He was a good student
at West Point.
Maybe somebody will do a photo of him,
if this is Philadelphia, or Windsor, or maybe it's Detroit?

●

I don't know what Jay Leno had to say about the
Persian
Gulf. But what an opportunity to be an asshole about other
people's
deaths. He probably had 2 or 3 lines every other night from
August 15
to January 15; & then 2 or 3 lines per night until late March. A
big mouth with those big ears.
Almost none of his jokes are funny but the
studio audiences seem to break up.
So we're supposed to think
he's
funny. The guy's got a face like a package of breakfast cereal.
What's

so funny about that?
                            Even that little kid with the glasses
who does the Heinz ketchup commercial, he's about 7 or so, is a
    much
better video communicator than Jay Leno.
                                    And Madonna? Well
        at least
Madonna's beautiful, and when you compare her to Jay Leno
    then you have
to say, Sure, she can sing, sort of.
                            But neither one is as good as the
little kid with the glasses.

                                •

            Or sometimes
I think I love the dead Confederate soldier in that Matthew
Brady photograph
sprawled face up under a gun carriage eyes closed mouth
relaxed the gentle line of the jaw pressing into sweet
Pennsylvania earth.
                        The soil
where you are born, or where those touched
you as a child were born, is part of your bloodstream.
It is March & I am flying over the Avalon
Peninsula. Over the Gulf/Stream.
                                Down below through
the grey March clouds
the blue is astounding
                        as blue as Madonna, as blue
as the dark blue sands of the desert under a Persian
or Mesopotamian or Saudi moon.
                                •

As blue as my 4th image the Louisiana
Gulf
        where an old man is tying up a rowboat with a piece
of rope.
            That is the granddaughter of the old man
dancing in a circa 40s roadhouse near Hamilton
on the cover of the book you picked up.
                                        He gets
out wiping his hands & begins unloading
4 crates of crayfish.
                I am at home again
with things I understand & feel comfortable with; I am not
being jacked off by a thousand eager & empty-headed
young newsguys
                        plus some well-intentioned Susan Haratas.
Takes a handkerchief out of his pocket & wipes his face
stuffs the handkerchief in under his collar & walks 150
feet to back his truck up to the boat.
                                If we don't sell
our trucks & boats to Europe,
                        who in the name of Jesus
will we/
        sell our trucks & boats to?

                            •

        Dolly Parton has a flamboyant *Vanity Fair*
cover, June, 1991,
well after the official cease-fire. She is sitting
on the shelf edge of an enormous tank
& almost spilling out of an expensive silver lamé
dress.
        They have a huge orange VANITY FAIR behind her

blonde head, & a slightly smaller red, Desert Form! across
her sexy knees.

          Dolly Parton
is loquacious,
she has big ba-booms, & she can't sing for beans.
She can't sing like Patsy Cline.
And she can't sing like Lyle Lovett.

                                            •

      At the intersection of the Dhahran-Khafji highway, an
equipment truck connected to the 82nd Airborne has built a wall of
pale rosy white bricks at the back of their truck. They have painted
a large sign in approximately 12″ – 18″ black letters, facing outward
on the white bricks. The sign says:

                P I N K   F L O Y D
                T H E   W A L L

                                            •

      Patsy Cline was a great singer.
She sang that song called
"I Fall to Pieces." She died in a plane accident
when I was a child. I like her voice & I think her death
probably means more to me even now than the children of
Baghdad, whom I think about,
but whom I find abstract. Lyle Lovett, well, he's a great,
he's a natural, he's a great singer. And me? I'm just a guy
who keeps thinking about how infinite the desert sands seem
to be, the amazing blue of the gulf waters, the hot sun, & how
the women hustle, herd, nudge, their children along, comeon,

comeon, hurry up, if you're not careful you'll get us both
killed, with little gestures & clucking sounds that go back
perhaps 2 or 3 or 4 thousand years,
long before the invention of mainstream Nashville
or the use of mustard gas in WWI.

•

POSTSCRIPT

This page is also a concept of borders. Obviously now I'm going to
talk about other things including social divisions, mangoes, the na-
ture of the self, death, sex, jazz, love, the erudition of professors,
darkness, gay as a phenomenon, bread, and the appearance of blue
moons over Dubuque.

Taking this page as a border is simply a form of respect.

MONDRIAN'S BORDERS

for Victor Coleman

            Mondrian's *Broadway Boogie Woogie*
[which the English for some perverse reason
pronounce bugee wugee
                        & this is not, one gathers,
because they've seen any of the remarkable photographs
by Widgee – who probably knew every theatre
& late-night restaurant on Broadway –
from 4th up into Harlem –
                        ]
                        was painted in 1942. The
Germans
            from whom Mondrian has intelligently fled
are pouring into Russia
& the Russians are dying by the thousand as they stop them
cold in the huge white snow & blow their heads off
like slaughterhouse chickens
                        might, if they had stopped
to think,
            have learned something from this painting. It is
a favourite of art critics, but it is not really about
Broadway at all; it is about New York as a set of grids
& according to Mondrian there is no poverty
& no stock exchange
                        it is all colour & music & *Oklahoma* –
pretty girls in flapper skirts perhaps, although it is 1942,
& perhaps they are drinking Pernod. Who the hell cares,

it's a great painting, isn't it, his only gureat,
& who the hell was Lissitzky – just some goddamn Russian
& probably dead of a head wound cf
                              Appollinaire
in that remarkable photograph showing the wide head-bandage
after he defended Paris from the Germans in WWI.

Around late June somebody up in heaven
must spill a tub of soft butter into the air.
Partly
the heat perhaps, & the way light bounces off so much
foliage & bright glass;
but this light which lasts into
late August, this light,
goddammit, this particular
Summer Light
makes the entire
city as clear as an endless astronomical circuit —
every ash, elm, maple,
every child dropping a strawberry
popsicle on the pavement & crying, "O poopsy,"
every Samantha slipping
into a loose summer dress & feeling that she's the most
beautiful girl in town,
even ideas, lost emotions, stray ends,
all become clear.
That's what you want
isn't it, Goffman. Clear?

PROFESSORS

Their tweed jackets seduced me at a tender age,
I was about 4½, and too adorable to break your heart.
That air of being between bohemia and the establishment.
Rimbaud's well-educated rogues in charge of history.
The average lawyer thinks Einstein was a mathematician
and Georgia O'Keeffe is a West Ireland county.
Their comfortable 19th century furniture also seduced me,
there were flowers everywhere at G's, geraniums and azaleas.
I wanted their wives to smell of lavender and sandalwood.
I checked the pockets of their overcoats for interesting
historiographic lint and crumbs of tobacco.
Their daughters have straw hair and play volleyball.
A specialist in the history of Irish speech idioms
taught me to appreciate the phrase as a floating module.
His wife had red hair that glistened like crimson pyrites.
Their good taste in Renaissance music is often amazing.
They have so many interesting & eccentric cousins.
I have always admired their slow calm reading ability
– Fernand Braudel in a long 5-day gulp,
just like a 17-course Italian meal.
Finish it off with a 685 page book on Vico.
You have to admire them.

Sure, I've got a brown paper bag
over my head
            with holes punched in the sides
for my Sony Walkman, & the eyes are drawn on
with orange & blue chalk, just casual circles
so you can't look directly into my eyes.
That's what high school is like these days.
The world is too big.
I only like my friends to look into my eyes.
So for the rest of Gr. 13
                        I'm studying Lou Reed,
taking him
more seriously perhaps than he takes himself; The
Cure, The
            Smiths,
Jane's Addiction, Iggy Pop
singing about Dog Food dog food dog food.
Someone lays down a simple drum&bass line,
& you start tapping your foot,
moving your body to the music.
                        Learning about reality
as we go into the 90s.
                        Sometimes these simple images
lift up & swirl like exploding
chickens & beat their blood-stained wings
against the folded walls of my brown paper bag;
or,
    in a different mood, Living Color appear

with all that great avant vivid jazz-funk flair
or Sinéad O'Connor comes on & settles
things down.
               After all,
these are songs
about terrible & also moving things,
the car accident dealt with
in a single line by The Cars; Fine Young
Cannibals question the nature of profit; Annie
Lennox or Bette Midler's depictions of love. With
a minimalism more extreme than Giacometti.
With gorgeous voices
to smooth the edges,
               an ironic back-beat,
raw honey & fresh lemon as yellow as the moon,
                     & music
to make your head sway.
               Sometimes I listen to
Sam Cooke just to get back up after the Carnegie Hall
performance; & then I listen to Laura Hubert
singing, "I'm So Melancholy I Could Cry,"
               which
when you stop to think about it
             is
an extraordinarily joyful song.

STRIKE

           I loaf on the bank with my shirt off,
                            socks
& shoes off too,
             & watch my friends in the afternoon
Simcoe sunlight moving their clear white hands
like passenger pigeons
                     pregnant with messages of love. We
have some cold pizza, 2 chickens, 1 qt. of B&G white
& a doz. cold Blues.
              It is about 78°
                       & some young kids
from the local high school are water-skiing – hunched
in that particular stance turning a far north logo
into a summer Ontario lake image. Their red life
preservers
            bob up & down above the choppy blue water
like red beach balls attached to Donald's back
                          or
Pluto's, or Huey's or Louie's or Dewey's. We can do
absolutely nothing this afternoon about Meech Lake
or the new constitution
                  or the striking PSAC workers
or even the letter carriers who refuse to bring us
our mail.
            Although they love us. It isn't personal. I
would have more to say about these events
                      but
I have a chicken leg in my mmmphmm mouth tastes good.

I am towelling my face & my eyes are full of Karen sitting
legs splayed in a black string bikini

> reading

a paperback of *Lives of Girls & Women.*

> I have let you

see us undressed & in return you must promise me
one thing;

> you must believe me when I say that the

bourgeoisie begrudge us even this chicken,

> even this

lake, even this ½full bottle of Monnet brandy
lying on its side beside the wicker basket. They
will never give in, and we will never give in. We
are like the lake, flexible, because we are immovable.

            The desire this morning, early, still lazy
with coffee,
                a clear blue morning outside, almost Aegean,
to write a poem about how hot it was
a couple of days ago – the question mark of a favourite
big shirt which has, yes, definitely developed a frayed
collar, plus, would you believe this, a rip under one arm,
but loose, comfortable,
some 1989 copies of *Esquire* over by the door
& some recent copies of *Vanity Fair,*
I want to keep the article on Jean Stein partly because
I find her father, Jules, the way those steel-rim glasses
sit so aplomb on his composed face, relaxed tension,
so interesting – yes, it was hot on Thursday, a clear
gelati limona day seen through glass
                                but
a sizzling butter day outside. You could have taken
a strip of bacon & laid it on the Queen Street sidewalk
& it would have fried in about ½ an hour. Marcus & I
go to play pool at The Squeeze Club, the balls roll
slowly, the espresso makes us feel cooler; & then when
we come outside the city is still clear & even paler blue
but the temperature has dropped slowly to about 78
with a cool breeze. High pressure ridges &
low pressure troughs. Stuff we can't do very much
about.
        This little drop in the temperature
is so pleasant, plus I won 3 games in a row & Marcus

is fun to be with, that I begin to feel balmy,
simultaneously light-headed & full of espresso. If
that piece of cream&dullred bacon you put on the sidewalk
down on Queen was up here on Dundas,
cooked to a nice crisp red, I would just scoop it up
with one easy arm as we walk along & eat it for a snack.
Instead we walk up to Giancarlo on College Street. The red
snapper with extra virgin is as good as it was
when Andrew M used to cook here,
but the veal chop isn't as good, they don't cut it
properly, it makes a difference to the way it grills.
You see what perfect weather & easy pleasure do –
they make the whole body into a relaxed tuning fork
for picking out accomplishments & imperfections;
too much balmy heat & espresso makes me long
for absolutes, Iraq will become a peaceful country,
Ottawa will reform a number of laws,
the missing children of Erie County will return,
& we will all live forever & be happy with the world;
if I eat ½ as much I will probably remain
just a shade critical – of the meal, the dark blue
awnings, yellow light; but I have soup, & I eat
the whole fish c/w an order of fettucine & tomato sauce,
when it passes into my system with all that lovely
oil & basil, I fall in love with the night,
the moon, although there is no moon,
Marcus, although neither of us is gay,
& all these figures passing along
both sides of College Street in the dark,
                                        although if
I were to pass them again in the morning

while shopping, I probably wouldn't recognize
the thick-moustached Lebanese guy
in the dark suit. Sure. Sure I would.

THE AMAZINGLY CALM FACE OF THE YOUNG
PALESTINIAN BOY

I'm living downtown again, & making money,
sharing for the moment with 3 other guys.
I go to
Kensington Market about once a week. One of the stores
has free-range chicken. I don't eat rabbit. But the fish
is good, & I buy oranges & purple black plums
& bright green avocado pears.
I was very moved by those
lines about the perfume maker you murdered. Poverty can be
attractive. Presumably he was a fairly poor man,
with a wife & 3 children perhaps.
Also the lime seller
out in the Jamaican market.
Everything which is truly
beautiful is to some degree exotic. Look
there's a kid
on pink roller skates curly blond hair elephant earring
& I'll bet he doesn't even know
what the word exoticism means. Poverty can be attractive.
Markham was boring.
I'm living downtown again & making money.
Sharing a house for the moment with 3 other guys.
Likewise
the Portuguese fish handler. I used to live around
here several years ago. Or the young Palestinian boy
selling brown paper bags
of lentils & mung beans.

I am vaguely interested
in what will happen when the Portugese fish handler's
daughter
            begins reading *Saturday Night*
or going to French films. *Moon in the Gutter,* for
example. Or when the young Palestinian boy
discovers me
                  & thinks I'm exotic. I am, after all,
don't you think,
                  a lot more than just a good mind
& a couple of degrees from Queen's?

CITIES

We have salami and Emmenthal sandwiches for supper
fresh fruit
mangoes and oranges;
I change the sheets and read the first four chapters
of *Broca's Brain* while you take a bath;
Broca was a man with a problem
he was devoted;
I look over at my typewriter and think about the essay
that I want to write on the autonomy of information grids;
mangoes are tropical
mangoes are universal
all mangoes are fundamentally alike;
the front brain is at war with basic ideas
but what happens when you can't get back
to the foundations?
                    We make love in the soft blue glare
of the television set
between the night sky and the pale grey broadloom,
I almost lose consciousness until all I can hear is
your voice murmuring over a million small white stones;
your nipples are rough dark strawberries in the profile
of the empty apartment with its large windows facing east;
the red oblong PARK PLAZA sign winks back black
this stained mustard building floating on a current
of earth – clear moon overhead   young mother   innocent
moon. The smell of potato salad and musk mango and musk.
Bruce Springsteen's beautiful New Jersey voice
singing the word streets over and over and over again.

The south is a rotten peach
these rooms in the night are cities also
where we turn our backs on bedlam and bellevue
and walk into America again – the rain on our faces
soft and cool,
            patient, unflinching. It is, after all,
the only home we have ever known.

STAMPS

       Charlie Parker would make a good stamp,
there should be a lot of votes for that,
& Rosa Luxembourg,
                 she's popular in Toronto,
& Orel Herscheiser.
              Frank Sinatra once sent Orel
a publicity picture of himself & signed it – For Oral,
like hygiene, or like Roberts.

Herscheiser – while he's still a hero,
before he starts losing, before the fabulous golden arm
develops some infinitesimal bone chip
around the elbow, some surreal flaw to defeat.
                     What's
the difference to us if the person on a stamp
is occasionally Belgian,
or the landmark might be Dutch, for that matter,
as long as it's significant. I would like to see Grand Canyon
& Smashed Head Buffalo Jump on some of the 2¢ or 5¢ stamps,
make them large, okay
buddy, with good colours, bright dusty roses & hot yellows,
they cost enough, go ahead. We need indigenous images also,
so now, in 1992, this is a good time to put Tomson Highway
on a stamp. Or it's not too late for Pierre Trudeau
on the 10¢ stamp in a black G-string trying to look sexy
& articulate. Or how about a real honest-to-god working girl

from Detroit, brown-skinned, short black skirt,
no fist in the air, just staring right out at you.

Those
         eyes. Level.
If you're going to put a stamp on an envelope —
why not put something on it with guts?

THE GREAT LIBERATION

When you walk into The Liberty
one of the waitresses gives you a big hug & finds you a table
where you can sit & order the Cab Sauvignon
which costs about 16 or 17 a bottle
                                    & you can relax
with your elbows on the table & lower your head
into a pool of interesting tidbits of gossip –
a story about a new arts group, a juicy bit about a
well-known columnist who has left for Mexico. And
you can tell *your* stories – go ahead
it's all here like a chic Kingdom Hall. But
I think I usually like the bar scene itself
better than the specific stories.
                                    The clear dark
light & the voices rising & falling & the smells
of Japanese chicken & cinnamon & Thai noodles
are pleasantly interrupted by a variety
of interesting faces, a girl with wonderful breasts,
a fey young kid he looks suburban apparently has
something to do with money & he looks hot
he keeps snapping his galluses wide yellow ones.
Everyone has a different kind of sugar
or coke. I don't
need anything more than this to get back up.

The summer weather up here is terrific.
There are green peas & snap beans to pick over at
Panharget Farms sometimes in the afternoon,
                                    the students
in my workshop group are really bright as clean shiny
new nails,
            the after-supper summer light is lovely,
but, I admit, there isn't very much to do
in the evenings.

            I was watching a PBS science program
½ an hour ago, but
                        you know, I don't really give a
flying copulative verb about quasars. I think
the meaning of meaning
                        is what you have
before you begin to think about – What It is.
Pagliarullo
hit a brilliant slow inside pitch for a quick single
& this *monzer* the size of a tank came down the base
line & gloved it just in time. Tough.
                                    But
Pagliarullo hits some nice balls out of the park.

            I'm still hungry; it's amazing how a dumb white male
like myself with several published books

& an exhaustive knowledge of contemporary history
can make a sandwich in the dark without any problems.
I think it's something I inherit from one of my aunts.
I buttered the whole wheat bread & put a little salt
on the rare roast beef Lilly
brought me from Schomberg.
                              While I was making
the sandwich I watched the darkness out
in the backyard.
                    There is something very comfortable
about rural darkness at the end of a long day –
up at 6 a.m., lots of bright sunshine, 78–82°,
4 meetings with students, 2 new poems,
lunch at the German Delicatessen
across from the library. I think it's
the completeness; darkness in the city
doesn't have that completeness
& of course it doesn't have the late-night hawks
& Toronto full moons don't seem to be even
½ as large.
              So after the sandwich & a piece
of homemade pie I picked up my jacket
just in case it gets cool
& went for a walk down the hill over the Boyne
River bridge for a late-night drink at Oliver's.
And again it was this comfortable, like a favourite
blanket from childhood my old buffalo robe perhaps,
quality of the darkness – not disturbed or diluted
with city sounds or traffic, & full of odd nudges
from the past – walking over Trout Creek Bridge
in St. Mary's for after-supper ice cream with my parents,
or that night in Galt when my crazy stepfather

tried to jump off the Grand River Bridge
at Victoria & Water Street.
                              Peaceful,
just the darkness, a few late-night hawks.
2 or 3 passing cars, bridges as calm as sculpture,
& the shimmer of dark wet rural grass.

PHILADELPHIA

for Jan Conn

          I have been thinking about Philadelphia
all afternoon, about trains and newspapers,
about gas stations,
about a job I used to have in a mill on River Street.
I sit around with my friends in the evening
and we talk about the same things, literature, politics,
sex, the Van Gogh exhibit at the AGO,
                              but why is it
that I am the only one who thinks there should be
a train to Philadelphia every morning,
                              O say,
around 7:45 a.m. would be good?
                              Or who misses
the sense of Philadelphia in the autumn,
and how it stands for something even in the middle
of a cold dark January afternoon?

          This is unfair, especially when you
consider that a year ago the central part of the city
was a sea of flames.
                    There is a myth that encloses
all these things and I am susceptible to that myth. I
phone Sam, and we go out for coffee & chocolate cake,
and then we take a cab out to the Danforth,
go to Esperides and have squid fried in a light batter

and sweet roast lamb with large golden brown potatoes.
The food is good
and Esperides is a warm room. Even the darkness
of the Danforth late at night
by itself fulfills something deep and important in me.
Still, even out on the warm dusky street,
hanging loose after supper,
our cheap dress shirts pulled loose out of our pants
because of the heat,
                              it is my perception
that something is not quite right. Even the marvellous
new Hydro building by Raymond Moriyama
at University & College is not as appreciable
– unless you put it into a frame :
Sherbourne Street, for example, and Philadelphia,
and that building we saw by Philip Johnson in Chicago.

HEY, HEY, MITCH

How will
I describe the darkness of Wrigley Field at night
& how people turn to each other
after a great hit & say, Did you see that?
                              Or the popular song
that keeps running through my head, "Your daddy's rich
& your momma is so good-looking."
                              The darkness
is a soft ½darkness,
The light falls on his blond moustache
& makes his eyes bluer, midwestern, cornflower
blue. He is with his wife
& one child, a boy; his wife's name is Serena,
Lebanese descent, beautiful, the other child, 4,
also a boy, is at home.
                    I am
by myself for a week; Mitch Williams –
                         not the
Bad Boy of postmodern baseball, I have seen him
in bars once or twice, tall, slim, good-looking,
laughing a lot; I would be more inclined
to call him the Iconic Hot-dog, in the Barthian sense,
of postmodern Chi City –
                      is pitching, it's the 8th
& he's holding a slender 3–2 lead & keeping them
hitless & witless. I am never lonely
when I meet people like this. His wife's eyes
& the quick way she has of laughing nervously

but with pleasure at an unexpected play
make our small pool of order a warm place
& the beer tastes that much better. "Throw the
fast ball throw the fast ball Mitch,"
chants his 9-year-old son. I say, "He's going
to hit him with the sinker,"
                              & he does, he throws
the heavy ball with a lot of thumb behind it –
drops it in under the amazed batter's knees
to get the last out;
                     & he himself, always the clown,
a tall slim good-looking guy who laughs a lot
in the bars,
             is bent so far over after the pitch
that he's almost like a crab –

                              legs stretched out
glove in the air, right hand fingertips touching
the dust in front of him, eyes locked
at that exact point where he placed the ball. They
are all on their feet yelling for him
& I am glad. I like this field better in some
ways than the huge cement skydome with its giant
retractable clamshell helicopter-focused roof. But
it is also those blue midwestern eyes
that say, "Comeon, relax, forget it, you're at home."
& Williams, of course, because he's such a fabulary
extrovert. What else can I say?
                              I am sitting
right in front of you. My hands are folded
on the formica table, relaxed, at ease. Every thing

in the world should be this simple.
                                    What
can I tell you that   you don't already know?

TAN

Amy Tan is one of the most gorgeous new
American writers presently at work. What I like
best about her work is its effortlessness, the way one detail
leads with a completely natural grace to
another detail about a young girl's choice of wardrobe
for travel. She has stories, in other words,
a number of stories contained
within a single box perhaps a white cardboard shoebox
sitting beside another shoebox that still contains
wrapped in white tissue paper of the kind you get in stores,
a pair of glossy red shoes. The stories are on loose
sheets, they are not bound together by an obtuse plotline;
rather, they have so much in common
that they simply touch on each other & develop their own
persuasion.
       The work I am up to my elbows in at present is
    more
centred. Tom's story, with Tom, even indirectly,
as the constant centre of reference; and the world,
like innumerable photographs, swirls at one or another
speed or F-stop in Tom's camera.
       So Tan's work,
listening to her read from *The Kitchen God's Wife,* is more
than good art or refreshing. I am actually liberated
by watching her concentrate on the good stuff, the fresh peas,
yellow corn, soft petalled artichokes,
& she casually throws the husks over her shoulder. The
beans & the corn are as fresh as if it had just rained.

Ontario is gorgeous in the summer. Northern lake fish like sturgeon are flown directly to the coast. With daisies in their mouths. We have a lot of manufacturing lay-offs, and more unemployed Phds than you can count. > Caribbean shrimps are supposed to be better than the ones from Louisiana, tastier, the man says, eat them in 2 big bites and suck the last sweet bit right out of its shell. > A pink elephant by Tom Thomson floats past on a street parade, Kate talks about some Steiglitz photographs of Georgia O'Keeffe. > We are sitting around a long table against the morning glory yellow wall at Britoli's, Frank and Paulo have their arms around each other's shoulders reviewing baseball, the bread is good, Carol is reading a letter to someone from her friend in Amsterdam. > Red Hot Chili Peppers are still a zany and classy group, this thing they have about playing with their dicks hanging out of their pants is wild. O'Keeffe's desert flowers are great. Innovative musicians, sure; but maybe a tad too aggressive. > We're splashing wine and eating soup. There are about 9 films out of 75 in Toronto at the moment that are worth seeing. > There are 100s of problems in the world. More. There are millions. People don't solve problems so much as they respond to challenges. > Paulo turns down a piece of chocolate raspberry mousse cake. We have all the elements we need. We are in the process of discovering a package. > Well, something more radical than warehouse sound or wide lapel suits. Caribbean shrimps are supposed to be better than the ones from Louisiana, tastier, the man says, eat them in 2 big bites.

I don't know what it is about youth
except for an honest desire to concentrate on textbooks
of infinitesimal calculus,
                              & at the same time a great love
of carelessness,
                    a wanton energy,
throwing their shoulders around as if ecstasy is movement
or motion is ecstasy,
                              a wantonness, a carelessness so
beautiful that like a warm summer breeze you lift
your hand up to your red hair
in amazement & open your mouth to taste the fine grains
of copper magnesium cobalt in the summer air.

In Tobacco Heaven my friends are killed
on freeways. Smoking dope perhaps, or a fifth of cheap liquor.
They are about 17, tall & slim,
                              usually wearing t-s
or sloppy shirts;
                    except for Carson who was short & plump
the class clown, with a flat-top haircut,
who went through a guard rail in a red Mazda
& fell 135 feet.

A boy with the body of a
perfect high school basketball star

long torso no waist & the smile of a sardonic angel
my name is John,
                    call me Johnny Slow Hand,
driving
with a large unadulterated jumbo of Coke
Joan Crawford's favourite drink.
It makes me nauseous, she once said,
between his long legs,
                    radio blaring Elton John
that song about how the blues will always come back
with brass in the background
                         a lift from LA Express
caught the tail of a grey Plymouth
making a lazy turn no tail-lights onto a country side road
& was then clipped by 3 cars & a truck
                                    & flipped
on the boulevard.

        Saturday night
the cars have to be cut open with an acetylene torch
to lift their once perfect Adidas-shod bodies
out of the wrecked car the way you would lift an egg out
of a crushed bird's nest.
                    Mostly boys,
the girl was an exception, & under the age of 29.
Boys have the big A-stat. A for accident
& A for a sort of hyper-tense anxiety
backed up by a tumultuous review of hormones.
Boys are expressive, sure, okay,
& also aggressive drivers.

Jerzy Kosinski
snuffed out with a plastic bag.
Surely you weren't trying to do anything like that?
When you're 17½ the world is a huge 6 / 5ths.
6 / 5ths of a gigantic moon.

                              Cut throat of the sun.
Slashed wrists of the moon.

                    You just put your foot
on the gas a little too hard with one arm out the window
& leaned back like a lazy greyhound on the comfortable
seat.

        Cut throat of the sun.

                        Slashed wrists of
the moon.

            6 / 5ths of the dark night.

          Tobacco Heaven lays out
the coloured highway signs from Thunder Bay to New Mexico.
Life is almost always beautiful

                              or at worst a bit of a down.
The upside on the girl is that she wasn't decapitated,
unlike the Hispanic kid who was
driving with his feet just to prove he could do it.
Can you do it Jaime can you do it Jaime can you do it Jaime?
Si,
    it is easy, I can/
                    do it.
And if you lose control
then the night road is wrong because
it has imperfect highway seals under the asphalt
some designs don't breathe the way a highway

should breathe. Some axles lock, & some don't.
Driving with your knees only is strictly forbidden
while eating pizza
                    turning over a tape cassette
or changing your shirt.
The Buzzcocks should never have broken up
when they were so so good. Some curves
in the highway are actually a dark blue parallel.
Some high schools have good basketball teams
with cheerleaders & some don't. All highway signs
should be *illuminated*. Some windshields
break more easily than others.

TAPIOCA

Mrs. Matisse, I say, when I get her on the telephone, Is it ok if I take Henri out for coffee? I know this is a different time period, time has borders also, but what the état, I think we can do it. Tell him we'll have a big plate of sweet *arrabiata* and I won't mention Claes Oldenburg's bright-coloured canvas hamburger sculptures even once. We'll just talk about Henri's *Jazz Portfolio* and questions of general focus.

He's out, David, she says, He's paying a bill and having some shirts made.

I wanted to talk to him about tapioca. I've decided that tapioca is the opposite of style. Obvious, I guess. Love is such a sweet bowl of tapioca. But it needs character. It needs wit. Something the French masters were good at, Pascin with his endless drinking, Dufy with his *crême brulées;* and it needs colour, the advertising photographs for style should be of baseball players and models.

So I go out for lunch around 2:30 – rare roast beef sandwich as usual, but with a slice of honest dark chocolate cake on the side. Dark w/ hazelnuts, I might add, and I like to lick a little salt off my hand before I eat the cake.

Well, stupid, my mother says, I didn't tell you to eat nothing but tapioca.

COMFORTABLE SHOES

It's amazing how easily I can turn the most
embarrassing remark around as long as I'm wearing
comfortable shoes,
                    Clark's wide last or Nike's court shoes,
whatever. For example, Grant walks over to me at a party
for Gord Raynor & says, Sorry to hear about your losing
your job with the Waterloo Arts Council. He has a nice
smile on his face, & he obviously thinks this is a good
bit to do.
            And I simply smile at him, very relaxed, & say,
I'm working on a new book, or I've just discovered a great
recipe for chicken with pistachios & red onion. And
I tweak his cheek, & give his collar a jerk,
as if to say, Why don't you buy some new shirts, fella?

How do I know he's being insincere? Because he's not even
vaguely concerned about me, we're not even real friends –
he just wants to make the commiseration & get the scoop
on how it happened. So why should I waste my time
telling him how it happened. It was nothing anyway,
it was just a wastebasket, so to speak. And I stroll
away to get a drink. I'm not a great writer,
& I don't put very much stress
on having a perfect history of proprietry,
although yes, I do like to have a shower every morning,
clean socks, a little talcum powder in a pair
of comfortable shoes. Personal information,

I mean a bite that corresponds to a sensitivity
you may have, goes for a sentence or two, sure; but
it doesn't redefine your good stuff. I've got a good
curve on the outside, that's about all I need.
But listen closely: you should never go out for
the evening without wearing a pair of comfortable shoes.

THE SKY BLUE HEART OF ONTARIO

for Ed Grogan

            Here in the sky blue heart
                            of Ontario
I am sitting on a battered wood&canvas lawn chair
out on the beach at Hanlan's Point
without a Citizenship. Behind me
to the north there are the lush Muskokas
& west there are the rugged boonies & farms
that begin before Great Slave Lake.
                        I am happy &
useless in my rumpled chinos
with a large double scotch
not reading because I would need a 5×8 portable
red plastic box light. After all,
this is an island in Lake Ontario.
                        The sun
is coming up orange; there are trees,
& the great smoke of Toronto is in the distance. I have never
believed in the Iroquois that much. In my heart
I have always believed the Sioux
to have been kinder
& to have had a larger concept of glory
                                preferably
sitting on their horses.
                    There is a bright 86°
for today. The sun is coming up orange. I have always
believed you want

to kill me with your stupid ideas
about Canadianism, but relax, I don't hate you for it.
I am healthy despite these attacks,
talented, & stronger than 2 average people.
                                        I don't
hate you for it; I just think we should bring
our horses down to swim in the Lake. It's warm
this morning, & I regard you & the cicadas
with a bemused & moody eye.

WARHOL

for Kathy Melanson

We think of Time generally as being abstract, although Time is the condition in which these cultural periods happen, which is funny, don't you think, because we say that Wittgenstein and Heisenberg are abstract, whereas they're actually very tangible; and then we've got De Kooning, who is senile now (Warhol copied him, well, he tried to copy his face, he couldn't very well copy his memories, Dutch, Amsterdam, hetero, adolescent lusts for French schoolgirls, the importance of Hans Hoffman, anti-Nazi, the *sturm* troopers in Berlin squares, where Alban Berg used to walk, trying to destroy the German people whom they said they loved, when, in reality, the reality of real time, they were nothing but a National Rifle Association in power; how could Warhol even copy his face, that gorgeous thick-browed innocence & those eyes), well, he's senile now & there's going to be a lot of litigation over the paintings. And of course De Kooning, being senile, doesn't know...well, what doesn't he know? Imagine if we could take a sortie into De Kooning's mind, sort of like taking a dune buggy into the desert, what sort of blue & rose & grey flowers we *might* discover.

A girl sitting in the front row of an OAC class where I'm doing a workshop this afternoon. I ask her if she thinks Joan Baez is a great singer. She's about 17, bright, high forehead, good eyes, attractive. She says, Joan Who? I say, Baez. Bi Ezz. She smiles, not defensively, let's not attribute things, but with a sort of natural mechanical amusement, and shrugs, looking around, reflexively, to see if there is peer group support. There isn't support exactly, but a sort of curiosity. These kids, it should be pointed out, especially since we touched on events in Europe in the 1930s, listen to 1000s of groups in a given year, most of them trash, some of them outstanding. Then a boy at the back of the class, in a black motorcycle jacket, says, Yeah, she's terrific, she's really important. He has status. He knows a lot about The Smiths, and that Stephen Morrissey isn't nearly as cool as he's supposed to be. They all turn and look at Jod, that's his nickname, and sort of nod. The attractive girl in the short-sleeved dark blue sweater sort of shrugs and slides down a bit in her seat. The class turns back to me with increased interest.

Don't you think it would be more interesting than our average boring, Here's a new writer from Belgium, and he's going to read to you from his new unpublished boring Belgian novel, to have an evening at Massey Hall, or Thomson (Thomson really needs to be liberated a bit, don't you think) with De Kooning sitting on stage, white coveralls etc. against a background of his paintings and some large blow-ups of black holes & red dwarfs, and to have Baez in the middle of the stage singing that song O when the angels come out in the morning and blow their trumpets?

SOMETIMES MEN BURN WITH A CRAZY FEVER

           "Honey," she says, "do you want to dance with me?"
We are in
         the dark meadow outside the Mackenzie farm,
there's a clear yellow full moon & she's standing
with her hands on her hips & her head back.
I'm sitting down on an empty box,
she's being cocky,
            here in a dark meadow
out on the Cedar Road,
under this harvest red copper hinge in a cobalt sky
not far from where we used to play as children.

         I know what she means. She means just slow
at first then fast then really slow
– like that couple in *Badlands*
dancing beside the parked car on their way west
one bank after another.

         She undoes her tomato red blouse
& her breasts catch the light like flowers
5, 6 minutes from the river where we used to smoke
brown leaf golden tossed crumpled cigarettes
& talk about each other's bodies
& why Paul wouldn't go to the school dance
with Esther.
"No," I say, "I don't,"

feeling my balls turn upside down
like a picture in *Gray's Anatomy,* Erasmus reflecting
on the history of Holland,
                              old Haarlem,
Jan Steen's painting *Girl Eating Oysters*
my balls turn upside down in my faded jeans
& go into my throat like a chicken bone
or a big piece of crusty bread. I have some
matches in my pocket. I get up & walk toward
the Mackenzie's blue & grey barn.
Tomorrow I want to reread *Day of the Locust.*
Tonight I want to set fire to this barn.
                                        She turns
away in the moonlight & looks back her face looks
like a famous painting or a great perfume advertisement
in a glossy magazine but subdued by shadow.
                                        Her sweet
brown nipples ache in my throat like bitter elm buds.
Her blue eyes singe the back of my throat.
I put the bottle back in my jacket pocket & keep
walking, head way back, toward the barn. Her skirt rips
at my stomach like a dark blue knife.

For example last night, it was Thursday, I said to Paula, "I just can't make the good things happen here." I was speaking of Tobacco Heaven, the city with the big stock exchange on the north shore of a lake. There was a large pot of soup on the stove. Paula is an old friend. She was sympathetic and made drinks. I told her I thought it would be better in New York or Chicago; New York is pretty gay, and I have always had romantic ideas about Chicago, because of Sandburg perhaps, that one poem.

And she says, "It's not working in Toronto." She usually calls it hogtown although there haven't been any hogs lapping up acorns down by the lake since 1790. "Maybe that's because it's a *big* city," she says, "so why try another one?" She sips her drink, just a splash of red, she never drinks liquor, but the woman she lives with loves Martinis.

"Small towns are nowhere," I tell her.

Paula is slim and wiry with short cropped thick ash-blonde hair and a smile as big as your shoulders. "Maybe," she says, "you're asking for the same things..."

O yes mama I want the same things, the same things to happen over again. I love to be enthralled, and I loahv to have my heart broken.

"Whatever they are..." she leers at me with a wonderful pleasant raisiny cinnamonny smile.

Then we got into tasting the soup, tomato & dill, yum yum, it sure is good with that calabrese bread; she gets out some black olives and some green olives, and I make myself another drink.

Carol would be home around 11, no point in holding supper until then. Paula says, "There's nothing wrong with the city, *Deuxmains,* a big museum, a great university, lots of art galleries." She calls me *Deuxmains* because when I come for supper I always have seconds. The black olives are good with a mouthful of red soup, the fat green olives are good if you let the scotch slosh around over them until you think of green birds in the jungle, lifting their wings and settling down on tables.

She says the problem is with me. Yo, I'm bad. I'm bad. I take it out of my pants and I don't know what to do with it. I wish to God I could find a decent teaching job at Louisiana State, and then I could go fishing on the gulf on Sundays. My other alternative right now is Algonquin Park, but I favour southern Louisiana.

"No," Paula says, "you're a really wonderful guy; but," she says, licking the soup ladle, "you're innocent, *innocente, innocente, innocente.*" Paula has an MA in Italian Studies. She says, "You're a small town boy, and you just won't admit it to yourself."

I once memorized the corporate histories of the 50 largest companies with head offices in Manhattan, and here I am wondering if I have enough money to go away for the hot period of the summer, so I don't know why anybody would call me a small town boy.

Then she leans over the chair and kisses me on the mouth. Warm and wet. That's Paula. Great soup, great smile. Guess I'm just an unemployed train man stealing kisses in the midnight tinsel-ceiling ballroom, after everyone else has gone home to frolic in the respectable dark.

OPEN HOUSE

The night air is clear and soft.
                                        You can walk
north of Casa Loma and south down Huron,
the people who gave us the word Toronto,
and think about anything you want, housekeeping
or Willem de Kooning.
The bag ladies are down on Bloor Street. The
muggers are drinking wine in Christie Pits far to the west.
You notice the renovated Edwardian houses more reflectively
at night. The
stars to the south over the Toronto Dominion Bank
building are clear and almost pale yellow;
the accountants of BrasCan are sitting up late at night
in their shirt-sleeves counting the month's receipts.
BrasCan is a multi-billion company with a base in Brazil,
where Carlos Drummond de Andrade wrote
the Charlie Chaplin poem, where African-descent Brazilians
invented the Lambada. This is Ontario. The grass grows
freely and the flowers are burning dark
as smudged coal against the unpainted wooden fences
in darkness. Cocker spaniels were the most
popular dogs in Massachusetts in the 1950s. Toronto
has one of the best music conservatories in America. I think
that butter wouldn't melt in the mouth of this city.

These are details at night; some of them
in afternoon light. A leaded window pane, a semi-Gothic

brick arch around a doorway.
                                          Victorian gable, chipped green,
deep flat cement window sills. They represent an infinity
spectrum. The cement porch where a painter was murdered
in 1926, the year that Hemingway published
The Sun Also Rises.
I am quite young, but some of these houses go back
to the 1860s, approximately the period of the Civil War.
The police used to raid a frat house on Lowther
on Friday nights in the 1930s. Whoever owns that completely
rebuilt house across the street has an extraordinary skylight.
The bourgeoisie are a problem. More so than the squirrels
on the roof of my house,
                                 or the raccoon who comes across back
yards from Madison and begs for pieces of bacon.

          The backyards are larger than you might
expect. Those raccoons have a fair bit of room. So
a large back deck gives observation.
                                          I saw
3 species of hornet, one reddish, & a pair of nuthatches
in May. I try to understand the world as it happens
around me in forms of light.
                                 The hamburgers
at the Food Works 3 blocks south are the best in Toronto.
Le Bistingo has one of the best bars in Ontario.
My Croatian friend with a festival mask tumbling
from her head has gone to sleep for the night
almost, but not quite, with a small white cup
of dark Turkish coffee in one hand.
I have given my whole life, okay, a big piece,

to the contemplation of certain images. And where
does that leave me?
                    With a large & very specialized
vocabulary. I have 47 different words for darkness
including *scuro,* as in *rosso scuro,* a *deep* red.
What do you nuthatches think? Do you think *rosso scuro*
is a darker red than those cardinals we saw
yesterday? I sit out on the deck after late supper
with my feet up on the white pine crossbar
& read back issues of *LIFE* magazine.
I suppose I could be making love, or going for a walk,
I still haven't seen *Ju-Dou*
or that new German film by Paul Verhoeven.

                    Sun streams through the front living-room
windows and makes patterns on the board floor. The pictures
of Willie Shoemaker standing beside Wilt Chamberlain
are a study of two different sports.
Willie is grinning, the mouth beautiful;
Wilt is balancing the ball on one fingertip.
The greyhound is the most beautiful dog in America.
They have long legs, deep chests,
& truly wonderful faces.
My favourite novels are very often
about people in new cities.
My friend criticizes me occasionally
for leaving criss-cross stacks of papers
on various tables, or bureaus,
& for shaving every *other* day, but we reach
an agreement fairly easily.
I am happy in a deep inner sense

like the comforter on the bed or
the peach on a white saucer on the kitchen table.
The Chinese family across from my backyard
have built an amazingly wide 2-stairway porch
out of fresh pale lumber that glows
in the after-supper light.

It was a good hour – we sat in the living room on the broadloom and had beer, and apple pie that Carol had made earlier in the evening. John warmed it up and there was cheese. Clips from Rita Hayworth's films but also 1000s of very effective still photographs with voiceover: New York, Los Angeles; Frank Sinatra, Aly Khan, who was quite a good polo player, Orson Welles, I like *Citizen Kane* but I've never seen *The Magnificent Ambersons*. She had a beautiful face and she was a great sex symbol. I enjoyed the film, I like documentaries better than a lot of feature films, but it didn't give me any special feeling of what it must have been like to be her, although all the guys, myself, John, Frank, agreed that those dresses, and she had great legs, were a key aspect of her image. Sure, Frank says, but what if she shaved her head like Sinéad O'Connor and put on some Wrangler jeans. Different period, says John, totally different period. I try to stay out of this conversation, I want some more apple pie, some ice cream, but Frank pushes it, he says he thinks Rita strikes him as being very much like a guy in drag, but, sure, she was having fun. I think he misses the point a little bit and say so. Carol says, Shave her head, put her in Wranglers, she'd still be one hell of a powerful woman.

Most of the women I know are into psychology, film production and, in one case, botany. She wants to go to the Sahara to study desert flowers. I might go too, but I don't think so. How would you feel about a documentary on Steve McQueen? asks Carol, she's annoyed, she picked out the tape. And I say I wouldn't bother watching it. I like a lot of American films, *Five Easy Pieces*, *Body Heat*, look, this could be a long list. But Steve McQueen was just a klutz, besides he was rough on Debra Winger.

RASPBERRIES

Paul Simon & Art Garfunkel,
when they were still together
                              made a song called
"The Sounds of Silence."
                         That's what my sadness
is like, dark, light,
                    I saw the video in b&w;
& it's like a bowl of raspberries. You know what a
delicate sweetness raspberries have when they're fresh,
just faintly bruised
                    & you pour Ontario cream over them.
Hello darkness,
             my old friend,
that's how it began. The song has a welcoming quality
to the first 5 words,
& then an effect of almost happy sadness. Art Garfunkel
who,
      (& look, I don't know if either one of them
liked raspberries, for that matter,
                                  maybe yes,
maybe no) did an excellent job of singing
the high notes on that song.
                           Art was disturbed as a child.
He had funny hair & he was Jack Nicholson's
roommate in Mike Nichol's film *Carnal Knowledge.*
Boy, are you sorry you missed that one,
                                      you know
you can still see it.

Anyway that's what my sadness is like,
dark, light,
                    & it's like a bowl
of raspberries. You know what a delicate sweetness
raspberries have when they're fresh,
                                        just faintly
bruised & you pour Ontario cream over them. I lower
my face over the bowl &
                          the fresh country earth scent
of the raspberries rises up to my big nose.
                                    Jack?
I've no idea of how Jack is,
he was really excellent in *The Two Jakes,*
although the reviews were poor.
But these raspberries fresh & almost as red
as Carol's undone tomato-red shirt
with the yellow leaf patterns,
the round bowl, the fresh Ontario cream,
                                    I picked them
in the dark with my bare hands, no blue&grey canvas
gloves for me,
                but I confess to a certain lack of
moroseness; I am constant but indifferent, & hungry,
so I lift the bowl up gently,
                          looking out at you
from under my thick eyebrows, fresh cream, no evening
gnats in this bowl
                    & let the raspberries tumble into my throat.

70

WHAT KIND OF MAN WEARS JOSEPH ABBOUD?

Summer's here & tons of light pours hot butter sun waffles through the big leaded windows of my dining area/front hall & the living room wide arch to my left. Always a good idea to have the living room to your left, I suppose. It's white, fresh, with a good floor & the sun pours in. I have a $7' \times 3'$ table that I bought from Wilkie, a friend, up against the front hall rad. Tons of space for papers, folders, unread books, typewriter, the works. Much better than the middle room I used for a study. I shower in the morning & work all day in my underwear. I don't need very much after all. Rent, of course, but not much else. I don't even eat that much in the summer. It was always my best time when I was a child. Steaks & mashed potatoes are winter food. So I'm regressing & advancing at the same time. I'm becoming slimmer & more relaxed & civil with my friends.

The trees are huge outside. Dark green. Good view of big dark green trees loaming up above houses as far west as Brunswick. Birds fly around. Nothing unusual that would interest my friend Carol. Starlings, pigeons, sparrows. The good birds, if you want to make a differentiation between colours or size, are outside in the back eating my Armenian landlord's lingonberry tree and crapping on his red '86 Buick Skylark. Am I writing very much? 8–10 pages a day which is probably more than I should be, but I'm in love, or impatient, or maybe just too sure of myself. I have decided that I am a man who was never meant to wear clothes. Dressed I merely exhibit the fact that I'm a largely unpublished writer, a genius, perhaps, thank you; naked, almost, I return to my usual more competent seraphic self. i.e. I am more creative. I produce more work every day, enjoy even the simplest meal, pace myself more slowly in love-making & sleep like a child.

My old friends, I love you so much. But every day I reject more & more of the tinfoil you have tried to pass on to me; & every day I become healthier, stronger & more, I believe in my heart, what my parents originally had in mind. Listen to enormous amounts of classical music. Spend a lot of time in the sun. Royal Comfort, & Calvin Klein. One slice of Steele's Bakery dark rye with peanut butter before morning coffee.

YOU CAN'T ASK EVERYONE TO PLAY LIKE COLTRANE

All those abrasively angry honking
tenors & hoarse
sad altos expressing black anger
& closing me out.
It pulls at my heart
walking through this club in the middle of a set
& sitting down for a drink before going on
somewhere else to eat. Because it is so visceral
& makes you think about intention.
It makes you
feel guilty for buying all those Joni Mitchell albums,
all those Tom Waits tapes,
all those
Ry Cooder CDs.
It's not just me. I can see it
on the faces of both my friends. We listen
& then drive north to a different place
before going to eat. How far down can J.D. Souther
get? How far up can Loraine Segato go?
We want
hot licks we want blue to be an ice-cube
gently laid on the eyelids we want brass to be
the colour yellow maybe Van Gogh's yellow
or maybe Matisse in a certain mood? As it is, we
don't even listen to Mingus that much anymore.
I haven't listened to that album *Mingus Ah Am*
for over a year or 2.
It's easy to slide away

from something you love
                              & grew up
believing you understood as naturally
as putting your wristwatch on in the morning. But
things change,
                    for a while, I guess.
We don't even seem to care if we're missing
a certain edge.
                    A certain perception is being
offered & we're missing it. My friends are
dumb white boys with good ears,
                                        & they seem to be
saying,
            "You're talking about the outer dark. Okay,
so where's the moon?"
                          You see what I mean,
as if
      we don't
understand the *idea* of falling in a moonless night?

LOST BUFFALOS

A New York friend of mine,
                              Paul,
said to me one afternoon in a bar in Jamestown,
"You've never had any buffalo in Canada,
have you, David?"
                    No of course not you breadhead.
No, he was a good friend. I said, No,
                              the buffalo
used to stop well south of the North Dakota border
in the 1720s
              & turn around,
                         sullenly,
& head back toward Bismarck. Where once there were
many buffalo, and no oil, of course; & now there is
oil; & there are no buffalo at all.
                         And he said,
"Why haven't you mythologized them? & don't give me
that 'peaceful capitalism' bullshit."
                              We were
drinking New Amsterdams with a plate of fried clams,
& I found it very difficult to answer his question.
              Similarly a friend from Montreal, Anglophone,
you know,
his last name is English but he speaks much better French
than that chinless wonder, Boor ass ah,
said to me,
      ·   & this wasn't in a bar so much it was in a kitchen
at a party in Scarborough & the kitchen table was a mess

of bottles & glasses & corks
                         & one wet dishcloth
I guess that was the bar cloth, he said, I don't know a lot
about the States,
we'd been talking Melville & Florida & Ken Kesey,
separately, 3 subjects,
we were a little pissed, a nice guy, but we weren't drunk,
he said, "I don't know a lot about the States, but they don't
have any peace movement down there, do they?"
                                            No, of
course not. The peace movement even turns up in fiction
for Christ's sake, & in films like *FTA*,
                         Steelyard Blues,
& indirectly in *Five Easy Pieces*.
                         They have peace movements,
sure they do, for sure.

               Sherry was like this also,
in several respects,
my friend the west coast film executive who gave up
on Paramount in 1982
& moved back to New York even though the rents
are astronomical
                    & you can't go for coffee
after 10, 10:30 p.m., a walk down to Union Square & west,
without wondering about the possibility of being mugged.
Sherry
had a thing about logos, stamps, money, flags perhaps.
Do you, reader, think these things are male attributes?
I'm not sure – I don't usually find that people
run to stereotype, or at least cultural stereotype,

as much as some people like to think they do.
                                        Sherry
would say, "I don't know what it is, it's not just
that goddam picture of the goddamn Queen lying around;
although why is she on your stamps, David?"
                                        And then
one night at a bar down in the Village after a play
by Arthur Kopit,
                    called *Indians,* a good title,
but compared to Tomson Highway's *Dry Lips Oughta Move to
Kapuskasing,* the Kopit play was a kop out, a piece of junk,
& Sherry said, apropos of Norman Mailer saying something
about cards, Niagara Falls, it does, it tumbles,
postcard art, Dadaism, stuff like that,
maybe a Duchamp card from MoMa, whatever, Sherry said,
& I think this is the film producer speaking not the woman,
"You know it's OK to have John Macdonald on some of your
        money,
but what pisses me off," she continued, "isn't a presence
so much it's an absence."
                                So we are into Sartre
or Wittgenstein or something. And then she says,
"It's the absence of Washington OR Lincoln
on your stamps. How can you do that? What gives you
the right? Even southerners respect Lincoln."
                                                And
I said, Look darling, my great uncle almost saved
Lincoln's life, so get off my back.
                                Besides I don't
think the majority of southerners do respect
Lincoln.

Harriet was a girl from Baltimore,
she was born in Winnipeg
but her mother was from Seattle, home of the Mariners,
who lose games & most of whom don't own
sailboats. We flew to Vancouver together
with her hand inside my shirt for most of the 4 hours
because she said the flight made her feel "queasy."
She was bright.
She had an MA from Princeton & then she switched to
psychology.
            But she
couldn't tell me if B. Franklin's parents were born
over here. He was 3rd or 4th generation, I think,
& she said, "I think American men are sexier
than Canadian men."
                  And I said, What? Sexier
than Donald Sutherland,
                  or Harold Town? You think,
seriously, that Dan Quayle is sexier than David
Peterson?
                  And she said, "O, you're always so precise."
She was curled up in her seat as she said this,
but she was married; & we were in an
airplane, I think it was a DC 10,
I keep track. And it turned out she meant
sexier than this one specific hoary scotch&soda cheeks
guy in the VP's office where she worked
at an advertising company
that did a lot of stuff for General Motors,
Canada Malting,
            BOAC, & the Liberals, they had
the advertising budget for the Ontario Liberals. She

thought Emilio Estevez
was sexier than this vice-president at the company
where she worked; & I said, Okay, Harriet,
okay, no kidding. But life is funny
& as it turns out
she divorced her husband & married
the advertising VP, slope shoulders,
soft hands, the whole suitcase.

Sometimes I think all these farms & highways
& major factories are about to swallow us. I don't mean
physically, swallow, devour, like
                                    an enormous train
accident. I mean our identity. Myself & Marcus & Evan
& Carol.
            We will have to restructure some of our patterns,
produce new national symbols,
                                    it will be raw at first,
a little bit like those red&yellow daubed figures
on scraped buffalo skin.
                            It will have to be different
than the specific myths of our cousins.
We should have our own flag, don't you think?
And our own national animal.
                                It can't be a buffalo,
they didn't come this far west of Great Slave Lake,
not very often. Perhaps a horse. Does anyone else
have the horse as a national symbol? California, Ga.,
Alberta? And.
                There are other dances, where you take
off the loose black shirt & blue jeans & the Argyle socks
& walk out in the fields just because you are tired
of the brass rails & the Mies van der Rohe buildings
& you are in love or you have a bottle,
one of those 2 things, & you want to walk
naked under the moon.

A LOAF OF BREAD ON YOUR ARM

When you go into Oliveto on a sunny
afternoon there is an immediate freshness,
the plump woman who comes to the counter has flour
on her hands; there is a smell of olive oil in the air.
Which makes me think,
                    somebody compared love to bread
the other day. It was Pieter, late at night,
at the San George at 666 Manning. We were all drunk
& talking about Vermeer & his goddamn loaf of bread.
Oliveto has buttermilk bread but I worked hard today
& I'm tired, so I pass it up for something more
substantial – rich sunflower,
flour-dusted crusty Italian sourdough,
Italian *challah* in great white twists like Rachael's
dimples,
            sunflower-nudged bagels thick with sesame seeds,
flat Roman *paddas* & the great sticks of crusty
Calabrese *baguette* which is almost a Pulcinello.

All of these breads have that subtle touch
of almost nutty olive oil. The breads
light up the store. I can hardly make up my mind,
they're all so good. A faint purple white glow
like the inside of certain flowers after the rain.
The air in this store is cool & sweet. I take 2 loaves
of multi-grain, 1 *challah,* 1 crusty *baguette*
& a number of cookies made with ground almonds.

What Aboud said in the restaurant was that
Dali's loaf of bread is more real than Vermeer's;
& I,
        I said, How would Marquez describe a man
sitting with his back against a wall
eating a loaf of bread with a pocket-knife
& a piece of Parma cheese?
                There is a touch of flour on one of the bills
as she gives me my change. Outside I rest the bread
loosely on one arm. Hector looks up at the sky
& sees a huge circle
of infinitely pure blue sky through the belfry aperture
of St. Paul's rainwashed granite across the street.
The philosopher who compared love to bread probably
didn't know very much about crops or weather. Bread is
bread; blue sky is blue sky; love is – in the eyes
of whatever person sinks their teeth into the other
side of this crusty *challah* & has enough restraint
to save me the remaining half. These entities all
complement each other, sure; but so would wet black olives,
tomatoes, morning doves, & Basque children running
through a field of wheat waving a burning fox
above their heads, and crying out Death To Franco.

DAVID BOWIE'S IMAGE

My friend Jean said she couldn't stand
David Bowie,
        it didn't have anything to do with his voice,
or the songs he sang,
           [I thought "China Girl" might have
upset her, because she's a literary feminist,
but she said no, she liked "China Girl"],
                      it was his
appearance, she said, especially the face.
                          We've just
finished, I think, coming through a period where men
have been all-out enthusiastic about beautiful women,
even if they do have careers, like Debra Winger,
or jobs,
        like Barbara McDougall; but women,
especially if they're career-conscious, tend to dislike
good-looking men
            especially if they're successful.

        I don't know if gay guys like Bowie
but a lot of regular guys do,
               especially if they listen
to a lot of music in the first place, &
                  are not heavy
metal fans, or if they're guys who have walked out
of their MA courses.
        Guys who have completed their MA

& are contemplating a doctoral thesis
generally regard
any form of pop except for the Beatles
that name alone would drive me crazy/songs that come
in a breakfast food box,
as being too superficial
because the songs are wildly unlike a textbook.

So what is David Bowie's image? Or
perhaps we should say,
What is the mystique,
or the debate
or the specific twist or bend
in David Bowie's image? Our friend Jean, & Jean
is both very beautiful
with classic moss-green eyes,
but she's also a very bright professor of sociology,
& she says, No way, *nada,* no,
she doesn't like him.
On the other hand millions of fairly intelligent
people buy his albums,
& his concert last year
at the CNE white elephant grounds here in Toronto
was a smash sell-out success with good
reviews.
Sally, a friend of mine in Alliston
& a talented writer,
once felt a touch depressed
about something & she spent 2 days & a bottle of wine
listening to Bowie's song "Heroes" over & over
again.

A recent feminist writer from Texas says she thinks the penis is very much like a banana. She has, she says, seen quite a few in her time. Not as many, I guess, as most women doctors. Rick's wife Dahlia got bored after the first 25, of course they weren't humping, they were patients, general examinations or something like that. Cocks are sort of amazing, but there isn't a lot of room for individualism. Cocks are not as individual as men's feet, for example, or their shoulders; or women's backs or their buttocks; faces generally take the individualism title, although several times in my life I've met a person who looked almost exactly like someone I knew. Hey, I said, you've got Robert's face, I wonder where Robert is right now and what is he doing? The comment about seeing quite a few, basically a lift from the dozens of Frank Harris types with their comments about

seeing quite a few puds, okay, and men sort of like these comments sometimes, more or less; gets a brief laugh from the audience. The laugh allows her to move on without really saying very much about her own image. I thought her image was in the direction of A woman and Arnold Banana. Hard-ons look pretty much alike also, I think, depending on the light, and some guys are a little bigger. But what's interesting about cock, apart from all the names for it, and sure, black guys have chocolate-coloured cocks and Indian guys must have reddish-olive and so on, is the variety of perhaps 20 or 25 different stages of tumescence. They are in that sense a bit like weathervanes plugged in with a special current to what's happening at any time, even in sleep, in the male body. Banana is a nice conceit, a wonderful colour: but that would leave out the most female part of cock, that almost blatantly pink bland glans penis. Mine has a small pale brown circle about the size of a piece of confetti, relax, it's a birthmark. The first guy I ever slept with was fondling it and then he looked up with a disingenuous expression on his handsome face, and he said, You didn't tell me you got married this afternoon, you've got a confetti mark. Hey, that's funny; hello, Ned, how the hell are you?

PIANOS

               Learning how to dance when I was 15
was fairly easy — there are no complex steps
except in your mind, and your mind is a dark space;
although some of the older kids were pretty fancy —
they would slide forward, put their weight
on the ball of one foot
                         and just sort of lift
up into the space moving with the music.
                              Some of my
favourite songs were by the Commodores,
                         Lionel
Ritchie's old group, and some of my favourite songs
were by Credence and The Band — "Up on Cripple Creek,"
that got us all moving.
                    And some of the parties
I went to would have a Fats Domino album
from time to time,
                    the same way I guess that you go
to a party sometimes and somebody brings out an Elvis
album, one of the ones where he sings "Heartbreak Hotel,"
or "Rip It Up," or "Blue Suede Shoes."
                              The Domino songs
are masterpieces of dialectical simplicity — one clear
staccato line perfectly balanced against another.

               He was easy to dance to, there's no two ways about
                    that;
you would just fly into the air

and do a weird swing
with your outside foot or a double boogaloo or something
on the last beat of each of those lines,
they were
that punchy. And then somebody would play Led
Zeppelin, and somebody else would play Bonnie &
Delaney,
and then around 2 o'clock in the morning
Joan Baez would sing that song by The Band
beginning with the line, "My name is Virgil McQuaid..."
But you couldn't beat those Domino songs to dance to
– they were so precise you could alter your own beat
and dance slow motion if you wanted to,
and then you
could speed up and dance faster than Muddy Waters &
The Stones. These songs never die never
die never die.
So play it again,
O sweet hero of my childhood,
I was thinking of you,
one foot on the pedal
a bunch
of yellow flowers in your hand/ Like a torch.

The red&yellow flowers sit on the clean oak table in a circular white bowl. These flowers illuminate the whole room. Okay, I exaggerated a touch, I pushed a little too far on the verb. There is an overhead light, a tall blue Art Deco standing lamp & a large table lamp that a friend gave me some years ago.

I take a walk down to Bloor Street & buy 2 multi-grain rolls & a copy of *The Life of Isabelle Eberhardt*, a book which Whitney, the girl in my novel, is very concerned about. Then I go for coffee with Jake at Dooney's. A strange name for an Italian café, don't you think. Jake says, "The world is changing so fast that it's upside down. You would probably be much happier if you were at the University of Chicago."

I am not an aesthetic person. Not really. I was born in a large house with trees in the backyard. Pheasants walking half-circles in winter. Yesterday we watched a film about 2 detectives in Paris.

Last night I had a dream about walking naked, I was comfortable in the dream, in a large tailor shop with bolts of dark blue & light grey cloth on the shelves.

I saw a fire once that almost blinded me. It was an enormous fire. It was several blocks long & the fire trucks looked like red & yellow helicopters, red & yellow whirligigs. I know nothing about the Soviet Union except that they have polar bears in Siberia, huge white animals that stand on their hind feet & nibble at carrots & potatoes.

Robert's not a gay guy and neither am I, but what does that mean? We're both straight guys, but we're not completely straight. These words are almost amusing. It's possible that they were thought up by rabbits in a think tank.

He's about 30, he's a television cinematographer, we meet each other while shopping, he lives a few blocks away.

He has a friend who worked on the Darryl Wasyk film, *H*, which is a truly amazing film; I've seen it twice at the Carlton Cineplex; it was shot over at Lansdowne & Bloor, Toronto is slowly coming to realize how good it is. It's good like half the time Fassbinder dreamed of being good.

He has a great face, almost a touch horsey but amiable with startling blue eyes.

I'm a writer, we've talked about that a couple of times, he reads non-fiction, *At Play In The Fields of the Lord*, and detective novels. He likes Chandler; he bought my book about Galbraith after the first time we met.

His girlfriend Karin is across the street buying supper; everybody's buying stuff: I'm buying tonic and both papers, I've been working all day. He's just bought cigarettes.

Pork chops as it turns out. I give him my recipe for pork chops – Smear them with Primo spaghetti sauce, a shot of lemon juice, and pour some white rum. Bacardi Light is good. "Do it in the oven," I tell him, "it's a lot easier." He thinks it sounds good and invites me to come over for dinner on Friday or Saturday, and invites Sharon, we've met him a couple of times while we were out shopping or at the Liquor Store. His girlfriend's an actress, or a model, I'm not sure. I say, Terrific, that sounds great. We shake hands the way guys shake hands after Bell hits a triple, except that George Bell doesn't play here anymore, he plays in Chicago now. Our eyes are very intent. His are blue. I've already said that. I try not to be repetitious. Mine are dark as the bloody night, but I'm attractive, so people say at least.

It makes me think of Gerald Stern's poem where he talks about swimming off the coast of Babylon, and stretching out his hand to someone who knows a lot about the desert. The desert is very beautiful, all that sand. We're both serious basketball fans, so I'm not sure which one of us does/does know/does know a lot about the desert. But what did Zane Grey know about the desert? He was a fairly sensitive guy, and intelligent, and he made it up as he went along.

PALE BLUE SHIRT, WHITE SLACKS

We sit in a large open bay window
in a summer living room on Indian Grove
drinking chilled white wine
in the middle of about 40 people we know vaguely.
I watch John acting like a Hathaway ad
for What kind of man *would* buy *The New Yorker*?
Welcoming guests & introducing people,
saying, Come and eat my chicken salad,
drink of me,
in his light blue shirt & pleated white slacks.

"Look at John acting like Harry Christ,
now that he's got the assistant's promotion,"
I say to my friend Bill,
"they don't realize that he's just a Xerox salesman."
You look at me & raise one blond eyebrow,
"Yes, but it's definitely a fucking colour Xerox."
And we both start laughing until our faces turn red.
Life is easy.
Tanned & athletic & young
slapping our thighs our legs spread like cowboys,
I have $3.45 in my pocket but the B&G tastes good,
you have a new Jeep outside but it's not paid for yet.

We laugh until our ears burn.
Our eyes almost burst with bizarre tears.

"Jesus," we say simultaneously,
"he does look just like Christ, doesn't he?"
Until our hearts flutter like turnips.
Neither of us is the new 4800 computer of sincerity,
but these people are *all* like automatons.
They all say – *Really;*
the girl can't help it;
the opera isn't over until the fat lady sings;
never give a sucker a Perry Ellis suit;
that's too bad, darling;
why don't we just go home and take a shower?
But they don't do anything except model expressions
& flaunt their 5 sentences about the weather.

            Maybe we're buddhists & we don't know it
but our big hands show it.
We just want to go to Tom's, put on some pasta,
smoke some dope,
& watch *Saturday Night Live.*
It's an institution because Lorne Michaels
is from Ontario.
                    John comes over with a large
bottle of red & fills our glasses, "What are you two
clowns laughing about this time?"
I shrug & he leaves for more wine. All I can
think of to say is, "Nobody here has any real ideas,
but John does look good in those white slacks,
just like a straight guy pretending
to be Perry Ellis."

My friend Moira
is tall & thin & with small breasts & a beautiful
excitable face.
               We get up around 7:00
& go to Andrew's house on Indian Road for breakfast.
This is Saturday morning before the ball game.
& Phillip says,
               "O you must try these waffles, Queen
Victoria would have gained 100 lbs on these
but they're wonderful."
               So we have waffles
with chocolate ice cream & champagne. It's a
celebration
               of something, & it's a great combination.

               At the ball game Moira is all over me,
she likes French kissing in the periods
where there are no runners on base,
                              Tony F isn't stealing
2nd with one hand in his pocket,
                              & the batting is a bit
slow. Moira is a computer engineer & knows her stations
& her stops. She would be a big Jays fan but she's
from Seattle
               plus she can't help cheering for Boston
because that Roger Clemens is so ooo good-looking.
Baseball is a way of relaxing. It's great being down here

with 46,572 fans & lots of sunshine.
                    Slow 5th inning.
                              Boston 3, Toronto o.
I love Boston so much I even like the word. Bah sten.
Toronto breaks the rule for well-formed names,

                                        names
should begin with a clear consonant,
then a good vowel,
                    then another clear consonant. Listowel
is good. Penetanguishene is great. Los
                              Angeles
breaks the rule a bit but it survives. New York is
good.
        Bath, where Chaucer rolled in the hay with merry
women of the church, is a great word. Florida breaks
the rule but it has that terrific D in the middle.
                                        Bell
hits a nice pop-up fly about 415 feet. They don't have
waffles with chocolate ice cream at the Sky Dome
but they do have a great restaurant called The Founder's
Club, it's about $150.00 for 2,
& they have truffled steaks
                    & *foie gras* with brilliant
green asparagus that makes your pee bright yellow.

              We leave in the middle of the 7th. Hot sun,
not much action,
                    & walk up to Queen Street. The
Horseshoe Tavern has great BBQ wings. Moira drapes
gracefully at the bar. Too much sun. Here in the cool dark
of the old Triangle where so many greats

have belted out the hits of our childhood,
                                    my wild
Seattle girl seems
almost shy,
              or tired, or tacit. I lean over & say,
Dessert?
              "Yeah," she says, swings one tight jean leg
over the bar stool. We drink 1 beer each,
sipping it slowly & noticing how much better it tastes
here in the cool dark than the Labatt's tastes
at the Dome.
              Then I pay the bill & we drive up to
Bloor Street for some fresh peaches
& take-out chicken.

CLARITIES

Nothing could be much simpler than this blue and clear white
nozzled bottle for misting plants
ficus bengamina elephant umbrella or avocado
sitting like a vase or a salad bowl at the centre of a plain
table supported by orange-
crates against the bright sunny red brick wall of our second-
floor sun deck.
                    I could go to the museum this afternoon or
the new show at the art gallery
but this simple industrial misting bottle holds my attention:
the sunlight frames it
illuminates it
fills the clear blue & white half-full bottle with light,
although it would somehow contain light even in a dark room
sitting on the pine floor beside the *bengamina*
or on a shelf in the bathroom beside some clean towels.
Part of this may be phallic and another part may be the
classic Bauhaus argument for functional form.
Phallic is possible.
I muse over this sitting sprawled in my khaki shorts on a
square cloth chair in the bright sun on the deck
looking from a distance like a clear object in space myself.
My left arm photographs the waters of my heart.
My right lobe is full of tobacco and peach trees.
The deep blue & white nozzle of the bottle is attractive
but the nozzle doesn't spurt water
it sprays, it mists
and is inexhaustible;

North America is full of phallic-shaped tins and bottles:
wine bottles
beer tins
bottled beer
most olive oil bottles and vinegar containers
even a tin of fava beans could be called phallic.
Dark blue is one of my favourite colours,
Galt night skies and union jacks and stars & stripes.
The bottle doesn't rival Rembrandt's *The Old Warrior* or
Vermeer's *Head of a Young Girl,* but it makes short work of
bad painting and schlock television alike.
Whatever it is sits honest as a piece of limestone
or a loaf of fresh bread.
Limestone and bread aren't phallic. I muse on the da/dunh dunh
dunh with which Beethoven begins moving to climax in his
     ninth
symphony and on the tragedy of Mark Rothko's butchered
throat.
Crane died young.
The human body is composed of one functional
shape after another. Stones down a hill. I am grateful for this
mass-produced $1.79 bottle: it is both pleasant to look at
and a perfect simple stimulus. It is clear the way I want to be
clear myself, although some parts of my mind are like the dark
water under a bridge.
My shoulders are red. The sun on the brick
wall and the orange-crate are also parts of this picture.

MASSAGE

She kneels over me and massages my neck
the thick red curls of her sex brushing against my back.
I don't feel like telling you how beautiful her face is
her thighs against my sides are as smooth as butter.
I lie on my elbows on Carol's bed with my head bent
calm but tired of being erect all the time.
Horses, an old girlfriend told me, can't last more
than 2 minutes; I told her I can do it for 2 hours
but I get tired after a while.
She massages my traps like a baker kneading dough
or the way you might play with a greyhound puppy.
There are myths all over America like sprawling farms
separated by highways and rows of trucks.
Plus I saw *Phantom of the Opera* last night at Pantages
and after the play we went for pizza and a 26ozer.
I am boyish she says and as irresponsible as a dog.
She strokes my bruised shoulder where I smashed
into the glass door throwing the fat bouncer
out of his own bar;
                    and I walk onto the moon
yellow Edam with white paper plane messages,
rich friable black earth west of Stratford
effulgent with corn, cattle and wild flowers
burning like fire along the edge of fences.
Our flesh is the light of this world
and I am bathed and healed by that flesh.
But I think now I will go back and plank my bahoola
in the steel seat of the John Deere tractor,

violets in my beard & a six-pack of cold Blue
under the wheel with the bright yellow corn
all around me
                    & almost up to my head. Her hands move
& darkness floats in dark water. For this moment
the white pillows and her touch are endless.

BORDERS

Board is one of the oldest words. Pale natural brown with a hint of pale green or yellow before they are seasoned. Sweet, they have a sweet fresh smell stacked in piles of 100s. The Romans made boards with axes & saws, stone ground axe heads, not the axis on which the green & blue world rotates. Boards are clean, rough & evenly splintered around the edge, and precise. Draw a line with a piece of lead. Cut along the dotted line. From Julius to "Little Boots" they had very vague concepts of borders. Gaul looked a lot like England, there was a Bay of Naples but Sophia Loren wasn't there.

The Romans knew nothing about America, or Norway, for that matter. America wasn't even on their maps.

THEY WERE MAKING LOVE. BUT THEY HADN'T QUITE STARTED
yet. She was being a little cool. Not cold or rigid, or playing rigid
like the other one, the snoot, but just cool, almost absent-minded, as
if her mind was temporarily at a distance. She was sitting on the
edge of the bed with her long legs spread out in a V, like one of the
back-up singers for Billy Joel, and he was kissing her shoulders. But
he relaxed. She had great shoulders, feminine, sloping, but not too
diminutive.

"You would just as soon not make love right now?" he asked her,
not with his mouth against her ear, she had great ears too, but
standing. The little girl was swinging in his pants. He stretched his
back, shaking his head, and ran one hand lazily across his chest. He
didn't want to get upset about nothing.

"No, of course I do, stupid," she said. With affection to him. "I'm
just not clicking for a minute."

He told her he was sorry, that he shouldn't have put it in the nega-
tive like that. Then he said, "Is it okay if I go to the kitchen for some-
thing? I just feel right now like something wet and sweet."

She had nothing on except blue jeans. She was sitting on the edge
of his bed with all this gorgeous black hair in corn braids and these
long soft sloping shoulders catching the afternoon light from his
bedroom window. She said, "Sure that's okay."

"Can I get you something?" The glossy hardwood floor in his bedroom looked as if it had been created, sometime way back in 1910 or so, what people referred to as 1st World War years, just for the purpose, or could you perhaps say the honour, of framing her long slender feet. She was barefoot, and she had dark hunter-green polish on her nails. The same colour as the Jag that he liked.

He went out to the kitchen in his briefs. That's all he had on, white, those ribbed cotton briefs that HOM make. The apartment was cluttered. He was living by himself for the moment. The kitchen was full of light, the geraniums out on the back deck looked like gobs of bright perfect China-red paint. He got a tangerine from the kitchen table. There was always a small row or sometimes a pile on the table, off to one side of the middle. Of tangerines, maybe one big fat lemon, 2 or 3 limes perhaps. So he picked up one of the tangerines, juicy and sweet, it was a big one. That gorgeous faintly-weathered, fine brown lines deep orange just a bit, a splash of pale green. He liked the shape of the tangerines, they were round and sort of elliptical at the same time. And they were juicy and sweet.

When he went back to the bedroom she was sitting almost exactly as she had been when he left. Her hands were clasped and relaxed and resting between her knees. She was looking at the floor. She glanced up as he walked into the room and smiled at him, a lovely slow lazy smile. The bulge in his cotton briefs had diminished a bit, so he looked respectable. He had the tangerine in one hand, half-peeled, 2 or 3 sections sweet in his mouth.

"Sure you don't want some?" He proffered the half-eaten tangerine.

"No. I want your tongue in my mouth. I'm just not quite ready yet."

She put her hand palm flat against his chest, it felt very warm and smooth to her, in such a way that her elbow was brushing slightly against the bulge in his cotton briefs, the kind that HOM make. The bulge increased. It felt good, he was in love with her, not always sure of exactly what she thought, but it didn't seem to matter.

"What do you believe?" she said. She took a small piece of the tangerine peel, playing with it with her thumb and 2 fingers.

"About what? About women?" He thought maybe she was talking about love, or the destinies of 2 people, or something like that. It was natural for him to say that. He was always thinking about women. His friend Jack understood that about Tom. He said to their mutual friend Henry one night sitting around at Pauper's, "Tom's a terrific guy. I like Tom. But he's just the way some guys are about alcohol or being busy all the time. He's no good without a woman."

"No, silly," she said. "We're not the only thing that's happening in our lives. I mean," she said, drawing herself up, pulling one foot up on the bed and resting her head against her knee, "what do you believe about things in general?" She studied him. She said, "You know, you read a lot more than I do. I know a lot about music. I read magazines because I'm interested in clothes. I don't read books very much. But I have beliefs," she said.

"Yeah." He rested one arm against her shoulder. He could feel the soft heat, subtler than the quick yellow Toronto summer heat outside, pulsing against his arm. "Like right and wrong. Basic stuff."

"Umhuh," she said slowly, "okay, sort of." She ran her hand up and down his thigh. Her hand was the colour of pale chocolate. It stood out against his hand the way an image you might see on a computer colour-modelling screen might stand out against some other slightly more industrial colour.

"You have terrific legs," she said, "strong."

"Not half as great as yours. Nobody would pay very much attention to me if we were at the beach," he laughed, he thought it was vaguely funny. "I have to put things between myself and the world, like books."

"O yeah," she said, drawing it out with her mouth, she was in love with him, no two ways about that, he was so bright and so dumb at the same time, how could you help loving him, she had said to her friend Susan at a place called Woodlands, a restaurant which is just down the street from Pauper's, but on the north side. "You just pick it up and do it. I guess that's how simple it is with us," she had said. She lay back on the bed very long and perfect and amused and wrapped her legs around him at the ankles, with her hands under her head, and studied him.

"I don't mean *ideas*," she said.

"Oh." He was very fond of ideas, and language, and books. He couldn't play a note of music. Well, not much, just a bit of harmonica.

"I love you," she said. She wasn't sure if she had ever said this before. She flexed her strong ankles against the outside of his hip, brought the big toe of one delicate foot over and tickled his stomach, just above the wide elasticized band where it said HOM. "So, it's important," she said. "What do you really believe."

"Like that guy the old man we saw outside of The Bay on Yonge Street," she said, "grizzled." She shook her head. The corn braids moved like dark butterflies. "The guy was on a little wooden platform, he didn't have any legs, and he was selling pencils." She had seen things like that before, and much worse things, but obviously she was disturbed by it. "What do you believe about things like that?" she said.

"Not much," he said. The bulge in his cotton briefs, the ones that said HOM, had diminished slightly. Legless, on a wooden platform, with leather glove pushers, it was a bad thought.

"I believe in art," he said. That was all he could say. "I believe in you." There was a pause and he stroked her foot. "You always want something simple to put like a label on my shirt." He became aware of the fact that he didn't have a shirt. On. He tossed another piece of the tangerine peel to her and she caught it deftly with her free hand. "Tangerines," he said, "you can put down, that I really believe in tangerines, like it's an example, an essence, it's challenging."

She lifted one dark eyebrow. "That's pretty general."

"They are challenging," he said. He held out the last perfect pale orange tangerine section with its fine white threads almost like a suspension for exact storage.

"No, I'm not hungry yet. My mouth's fine, we can have supper afterwards."

He tossed the handful of tangerine peel casually on the bed, put his free hand back on her foot, and looked at the last faintly glistening tangerine section in the afternoon light.

"No, it is challenging," he said seriously. "Most people just don't appreciate it. Gord Robertson over at Coach House Press understands it a bit. Matisse, you like Matisse, sure, Matisse felt the challenge but he didn't respond to it. Maybe he would have had to turn to photography or something, but he didn't respond to it."

There was that moment in the afternoon air, they seemed to have talked about it. It didn't seem to make any difference if he ate the last section of tangerine or not. His mouth felt rich, full of tart and sweetness at the same time. He swallowed. She had her long feet, one above the other, like dark birds climbing a tree in the early morning, some fancy northern residential backyard north of the Annex, resting comfortably on his stomach.

"Sure you don't want this?" he said, shifting his weight and looking around for a clean piece of paper or something on the bedside table to set it down. After all, you don't want to pick up a fresh tangerine section after making love and put it in your mouth with a little dust on it, or a speck of ash. They were both smokers, she just a few cigarettes, he quite a bit more.

"No," she said, "let's make love." She snapped the large dome fastener at the top of her Klein fly.

"I was just a little sleepy," she said, "I was just waking up after our nap. Don't get ideas," she said. "I always want you in me."

THE SKATE

IN APRIL 1969, MY FATHER GIACOMO DIED. THAT'S MY MIDDLE name, Giacomo, pronounced Jackamo, my first name is Tom. They phoned me at Harvard – the 3rd floor phone at Coolley Residence – and told me he had fallen from the 34th storey of a bank building that was under construction in downtown Toronto. He hated banks all his life; it seems to figure that it would be a bank that destroyed the tall beautiful slab-shouldered mass of my father.

I was back from Boston for about 2 weeks for this reason. It was earlier than spring break, I can't remember how much earlier; when spring break came I went to Virginia with my friend Sam, and we picked up long-legged Virginian girls all of whom seemed to have long sandy brown hair that looked as if it had been washed fresh in the ocean. And we went to off-highway late hours places. So Toronto seemed an emphatic contrast, not to Boston so much, or to Harvard Yard, but for sure, overcast and low-pressure zone fluctuant Toronto in early February, as if all the Toronto millionaires were worried about losing their steel and lumber money, it seemed different, different from the last time I'd been home, it seemed gloomy.

But this story isn't about me, it just starts with me because I'm sitting here in a pair of chinos rolled ½way up my calves because I spilled water on the cuffs and 2 pints of warm beer.

This piece is really about this funny kid I met on Queen Street West the 3rd or 4th night I was home. The kid's name is The Skate. He's about 19 years old, maybe a year younger than myself, not very preppy. I'm from a working class background, maybe a few hundred years, Tuscany, Calabria, on each side for all I know. Maybe a bishop or a cardinal tossed in to the Jackson Pollock dripalama. But, according to my old high school friends, when I see them, which isn't much these days, I'm preppy. They think I'm preppy with a capital P. I talk differently than I used to. I dress differently than I used to. I'm at Harvard. I wear corduroys and desert boots in the winter. I don't wear galoshes. I wore workboots, Kaufman's, from Ontario, to my classes in 1st year, true, but that was just the one year. I open doors for girls, if they're not already throwing themselves through the door in the first place. And I quite often wear a pullover tossed over my shoulders. In the spring. Which, actually, is something Italians, working class or otherwise, do a lot, in Rome, in Milan. This month in Toronto it was not spring, it was overcast, and there was no freshness.

O yeah. City of death.

Anyway I bumped into this guy in a bar called Madcaps. It was very crowded. We got talking and then we sat together. Blew smoke in people's faces, talked about Queen Street, about new bars, places I hadn't been on any of my trips home, 3, I think, in 3 years, and argued a bit about philosophers. He said Nietszche was something else, and I said O yeah, I'd taken Nietszche in 1st year, at Harvard, and it was nice, I said he wrote very well, but I didn't think it was a complete way of looking at the world. Then I was down on Queen Street again to buy some tapes to take back with me, and I ran into him again, and he said, Okay, you're buying some tapes, well, that's where I work, Atlas Records, you should have come over and bought them at the place where I work.

Now he says, I'm going to have a hamburger, you want to come?

"I've got a date."

The Skate is a real Toronto street kid, he's hip, he has a certain kind of manners, he's into culture in a sense, but he doesn't have any more education when you come right down to it, than one of the Dead End Kids. He himself probably perceives the idea that his life may indeed be a Dead End by the time he's 30, but he probably doesn't believe his own perception.

He's tall, about 5′11″, a bit shorter than I am, with a very sleek wedge-shaped face, black hair cut in a flat-top, he's very exuberant, I'm not sure if that's why they call him The Skate, he seems to like the nickname. "You going to the opera?" he says with a big grin and an arch smile.

"No." His simple gesture makes me conscious of the striped shirt, the tweed jacket under my overcoat. I'm only 20, for Christ's sake, Albertini, save me.

I feel like spending some time with him, hanging out, and this could be the solution to my not wanting to get stuck up at Fran's Rosedale friend's for dinner where there will be remarks and comments, condolences, about my father. I have no desire at this time to talk to anyone about my father. Maybe one of the Queen streetcar drivers on a late run to east end Neville Park. I felt at home getting up for breakfast at Grace Street. I felt out of place at the uncle's. I feel out of place on Queen Street West.

I have 2 great desires at this moment. I would like to lean over and kiss him on the mouth, this other boy, this guy with a funny nickname, I don't even know. And I would like to get on a plane and fly back to Harvard, toss my battered overnite bag on the bed, and go out to the library for the evening.

I say, "Why don't you come to this place I'm going for dinner, it's a friend's, and then we'll check out a couple of these clubs you were talking about."

The Skate is a very enthusiastic guy. He says, "Sure, okay." He thinks. "We can go eat, and then we can go to RPM. That's a good spot. It's a bit trendy," he says, "but it's a good spot, and Red Ryder's at RPM this week."

"So that's cool?"

"Sure. I'm easy. Where do we eat?"

I haven't seen that much of my sister and my brother over the last 2½ years or so. This friend of Fran's who lives up in Rosedale is somebody I haven't met. Fran is still single but she's engaged, and she seems to be hanging around with a fairly crisp, respectable financial bunch of people, these days, which is what her fiancé Ned does, he's a bond salesman of some kind.

We get a black&orange Diamond cab outside Zaidy's. Getting into the cab, I can't help thinking how the soft stream of flickering lights, looking west, is like an inviting picture. Some girls come past with their coats open, office women, late 20s, probably suburban.

"Where to, guys?"

The driver is a laconic dude in his early 60s maybe. He has wispy grey hair tucked under a tweed cap. I give him the address on South

Drive and tell him we want to go along Queen up Yonge Street and along College to Jarvis, so I can go past Maple Leaf Gardens where I heard Eric Clapton play, Neil Young, other heroes, when I was 16, 17. And then up Jarvis.

"It's somewhere in Rosedale," I say to The Skate.

He says, "That's okay, I don't mind. Is this your sister, or a friend?" I tell him about Fran, and that it's a girlfriend of her's. I don't mention anything about my father.

"Okay," the driver says as we go along College, "I'll go up Jarvis."

"Yeah," says The Skate, who at one point apparently thought I wasn't from Toronto originally, "then you're up Mount Pleasant and you can go in from the east side." He can't remember the street to turn in off, but he seems pleased.

"Great," says The Skate, "I love Jarvis. It used to be even better, before they cleaned it up so much, CBC, dainty little French restaurants."

"Yeah," I say as we sweep through Bloor Street and onto northbound Mount Pleasant, "it's cool."

It's a trim 2½-storey brick&cement-front renovation on South Drive. I think Fran's friend and her husband have just bought it, or just done it over, one of the two. I pay the driver and give him a dollar, and we walk up to the front door, snow shovel leaning against black iron railing, and knock.

The young woman who comes to the door, extraordinarily lustrous bouncy bobbed ash-blonde hair, looks as cool and beautiful as a perfect lemon sherbet bombe. She looks at me enquiringly, taking in The Skate with the far corner of one entrancing light blue eye. "Yes," she says.

"You're Fran's girlfriend." She purses her lips. I'm smiling, I'm fairly good-looking, this is an expensive overcoat. She runs that beautiful pulpy tip of the middle upperlip over her bottom teeth. "Noooo," she says. "I'm sorry," I say, "I'm Fran Garrone's brother, I'm up from Boston, she gave me the address and said to come here for dinner."

"Oh, God, yes, Fran. Fran," she says, "of course. You're her brother?"

"Right," I say, "this is a friend of mine, his name's Gene, you know, like Gene Autry." I'm probably thinking of the club we're going to go to after we have dinner, RPM, south Toronto after dark, Red Ryder and all that jazz.

"Sure," she says, "come in. We're just having some drinks."

Fran was in the living room, sitting with some other people on one of two white sofas, looking a shade tired. She introduced me to her friend, Beverly, the husband was in the kitchen talking stocks&bonds, and we sat around and drank some fairly polite sherry. The Skate was interesting to watch in this context. He seemed very pleased with it. He was careful as he sat down in what looked like an antique Windsor armchair, he crossed his legs nicely, smoothed his somewhat skunky blue jeans, leaned back and laughed at appropriate jokes. Several people asked him what he did, and he told them he was in records and looking for a position with RCA or one of the smaller labels. It all went very smoothly, and it sure took a lot of attention away from me. Several people asked me, When do you graduate? And I said Oh, a little more than a year from now.

I talked quite a lot over dinner, nice long dining room, refectory table they said they bought in Bracebridge, Ont., with the woman who had answered the door. Her name is Enid. I'd always thought that was a wildly old-fashioned name, Enid, Edna, Edith, like Winnifred sort of, or like Harriet. Now the name has a warm quiet flush for me, like somebody blowing the dust off a really attractive pink pale green & peach lithograph so to speak.

I didn't talk to Fran at all over dinner, maybe a few words at one point; but The Skate, after some of the wine Bev's husband was passing around and extolling, he'd bought a case of it in New York through some big jobber up in the Bronx, became passionately animated.

He did imitations of TV stars, really droll stuff, he did Geraldo, he was good at that, he did Jay Leno and made a couple of remarks about Italians, forgot himself I guess but so what, I don't regard any guy with an Italian last name as being Italian, Bobby De Niro is Italian, Frank Sinatra's Italian, Liza Minnelli is Italian, they're symbols of passion and excellence, he didn't do Rocky Balboa but he did Johnny Rotten and he did him to a blister, as they say, used lots of 4-letter words, talked about Johnny Rotten, the lead singer for a group called the Sex Pistols, cutting off his hemorrhoids with a razor blade and so on. Fran's mouth fell open, I think she was shocked that I would arrive with somebody like this, he's a nice guy, actually, during a period of mourning. That's what Fran thinks she's in, an official period of official mourning. Bev's husband looked a bit perplexed but he seemed to think The Skate was funny, like a comedian on television, and Beverly seemed very amused.

"Your friend, ah, drinks a bit?"

I turn to Enid and shake my head. "No, I don't think he's drunk, I think he's a bit gone in the hopper." I tapped my head by way of explanation.

"Oh," she says, nodding, playing with her dessert spoon. It was quite a well-set table. She smelled of grass and flowers. I felt like leaning over and kissing her shoulders. It's winter but she has a wide neck dress that almost comes down over whichever shoulder she lowers. Handy kind of dress to have I expect.

I began to feel drunk myself around 9 o'clock. They were all talking at once, up and down the table, I'm not sure if The Skate was still in full swing or not. I felt drowsy, just one of those passing hits, and then you blink your eyes for a minute and you feel fresh, more or less, again.

I excused myself to this lush flower of Toronto bourgeois womanhood, Enid, and went upstairs to the washroom. There was a study or TV room, I think, it was a TV room, with its door open, on my way down the hall to the can.

In the john I look at myself in the mirror and shake my head. Poor Tom, you look glom. A friend of mine in high school used to say that if I had a really serious look on my face. Glom for glum, joke, okay? I was going to wash my face, cold water, nice big basin, fancy taps, but I thought it might make me feel like throwing up, hitting the wild beets, making a phone call on the big white porcelain telephone. So I had my slash, watered my gator, as they say, and just drank a handful of the water. It tasted good, very clear and cold, after all the warm red wine and smoky conversation downstairs around the table. "So that's cool," I said to the mirror, thinking of Enid downstairs. She had said, sure, that would be nice, when I asked her if she'd like to see a film tomorrow night.

Walking back along the big red hall carpet, I stand in the doorway of the TV room/study looking at things, prints on the wall, that stuff. There is a yellow&blue jersey, sporty, just a cheap jersey in coloured sections, lying on a small leather couch. I can't imagine whose it is. Too big for the husband, sometimes women wear deliberately oversize jerseys or shirts or t-s. I walk over and pick it up, throw it up in the air, let it fall like a pizza chef in the big front window of Massimo's on College Street, near the Diplomatico and the Sicilian Ice-cream Parlour. Yellow and blue, rah rah rah. Those were the colours at my high school, where when I was really hot in Grade 12 and OAC, I would go into games in the evening and they couldn't stop me, I would be up in the air, one foot way out moving around somebody without touching the ground, I would go around, I would fake, pass over my head without looking, don't look back don't look back, I would go right over them if I couldn't fake and weave around, up up up and hit that basket, I can still feel the slight change of air, fresh, hot at the same time, as you come down bouncing on the hardwood and break back into the game.

And over there in the bank of spectator seats, when I glanced over after making a spectacular play or sinking the ball, perhaps, would be my father. Giacomo. Always sitting hunched is not quite the right word, splayed perhaps, forward, elbows on his knees, but easily the tallest man sitting there among the other, mostly Anglo, parents. His lank greying hair would be pushed back from his forehead and ears, a bit sloppy around the collar, and he would have his work clothes on, those dark green workpants, or those pale tan pants he wore a lot. And he would have a windbreaker. Sometimes there would even be, and I swear that even with sweat in my eyes and a sore rib and my heart pounding, I could see it from where I was on the floor, a splash of cement, or grease maybe, or paint, on his pants. He would have that big soulful but tough fleshy expression on his face, thick eyebrows jutting out a bit over his eyes. And he would have a dead half-smoked cigar in one hand dangling beside his knee.

I ball the blue&yellow jersey, soft, heavier than the shirt I used to wear over my shoulders before going on the court, into a sort of blue&yellow puppy, I jam it a bit between my fists. Then I bury my face in it, smelling I don't know what, a woman's perfume, cigar smoke, not sweat. The room goes completely dark. Naturally, I'm blind, right. I can feel this big jagged thing like a tin-can lid coming half-loose in my stomach, up around my chest, where the heart pounds. My mouth feels dry, and my eyes are wet. I wipe the crumpled balled-up jersey across my face and eyes. Catch a trace of it. But I don't cry, still staring down into the crumpled big flat ball of a jersey. Boys don't cry. I wish I could, Jackamo, Jukamo. Truly and really. But I can't.

PHOTOGRAPHS OF SINÉAD O'CONNOR

I THINK I KNEW THAT SARAH WAS GOING TO MARRY SOMEBODY else the first night we slept together. We fell in love at my friend Pete Carter's birthday party. It was at his parents' place on South Drive, there were 2 big living rooms and a huge French provincial kitchen that gave onto a large backyard green as glass dark. This was when we were leaving college. I think it was a *rite de passage.* She was in 2 of my classes at Trinity College, we had noticed each other a lot but we had never really talked. She was sitting on a couch by herself in the front living room tilting a glass of beer and looking very aesthetic. Maybe the French comes from the fact that the Carters had this big French kitchen.

I remember we sort of lost each other somehow after we got into the swing and anarchy of the evening. There was a savage discussion about Jean-Paul Sartre and Simone de Beauvoir going on in the blond oak rec-room downstairs in the basement. Somebody had put a girl's bra on one of the moose heads. I don't know where Cart's father got those moose heads. I don't think he shot them, he's a big red-faced plump guy, he's a corporate lawyer, he's bland and pleasant but he doesn't talk very much. I don't think Mrs. Carter shot them, maybe it was her father, so it's a sort of class-perpetuation kind of thing. And there were pale green squash pies laid out on one of the kitchen counters. Nils Effren and his friend Doug were doing coke over and over, they were making it last, doing it in very small hits, in the ground-floor washroom, and Carter told them to get their ass downstairs into the basement can because there were respectable people lining up and wanting to piss. But we started talking and important things were said, over large amounts of food out in the kitchen, late, sometime before the party ended. And we stayed up and drank coffee and small glasses of brandy or Grand Marnier or something until around 4 or 5 in the morning.

We went out together maybe once a week or so for the first couple of weeks and then we slept together for the first time. It was summer, school was over, everything seemed wide open. I was planning on staying in Toronto for most of the summer, but I was going up north with The Cambodian Rebels, a punky homemade group from East Scarborough. I've got a BA in pre-meds now, which I think is pretty useless. I'm not sure if I can possibly fight my way through 3 years of med school. And stay sane. It seems unlikely. So I've got a degree, and I've got thousands of photographs, I'm a photographer I've decided that's what I am, so I've made a basic life decision fairly early when you come right down to it, come on, admit it, I've been clear and decisive. All my photographs are punk, of punks, of musicians, of clubs, specific neon signs, ones I like, I climbed 15 storeys of the Grover Hotel in Detroit, up the back stairs to an equipment room where there was an open window just to get a shot of a huge 6oft pink&skyblue flamingo that was on a Dutton Travel Lines building down the street. I could have taken the elevator, I could have tried to use a pass from the front desk and shoot from an unoccupied room, or the roof perhaps, but no, it just wouldn't have been the same thing. It wouldn't have been an adventure, it would have lacked principle, it would have been cheap and vulgar and commercial. I got my photograph.

She was going away for August, to England, to see her mother's parents and go to plays and go hiking, the same time I was slated to go up north with The Cambodian Rebels, so we fit together like two perfect design concepts, I said to her, and she said yeah, we make sense.

We went out together maybe once a week or so for the first couple of weeks and then we became a serious couple. That means we felt seriously about each other. I'm not really sure what else it means or meant. We clicked in a big natural way, as if she were something I'd always wanted, and as if I were someone she just couldn't get enough of, or couldn't see too much of. We talked about going to Ireland together, we talked about going to Italy together. We had great sex, we went out with other people quite a bit, I almost had an accident with her father's car, but, I didn't, I didn't roll it, it was on 2 wheels for what seemed like an unusually long time going around a very long curve on the way to Grand Bend one afternoon, but I didn't roll it.

It was great. We were great. That's what we said to each other, sitting up in bed with the last of our wine, talking after making love, and slowly working our way through her massive album collection. Blues, Dylan, Baez, Randy Newman, a Dory Previn album I'd never heard before.

We almost never spent time at my cluttered 2nd floor apartment down in Kensington Market. Because of my roommates, both of whom were slobs, that's true, or for some other reason, whatever.

But she would ask me questions sometimes about the groups I was listening to. She would say, Well you like the Sex Pistols. How can you listen to stuff like that? They just bray, like donkeys. And I would say, O well, I listen to a lot of odd stuff. I think, when I look back on this, that in some respects she didn't really believe that I took all these punk groups seriously. She would probably say to one of her girlfriends, O well, Doug just has these vague secondary interests, you know, not affectations, but yeah, sort of like affectations. Whereas the truth is, I like a lot of punk. I don't like any garbage punk, I get tired of really good stuff after listening to it for too long, but, in general, O yeah, I like a lot of punk.

We were having dinner at a little place down in the Yorkville area, they call it Yorkville Village, which is really a bit trendy, it's not a village, for Christ's sake, it's just both sides of 2 east/west streets and a small section of Avenue Road, where the new Dakota apartment building is going up, if New York has a Dakota, which is old and grainy and atmospheric, then we have to have a Dakota, which will be new and perfect with lots of new sandstone techniques and techy hunter-green steel exposed and so on, but anyway, it's an okay area, this was a restaurant called A Passy, with an outdoor patio, and we had had some very good chicken.

They had fresh peaches with raspberries on the menu and I asked the girl if I could just have a bowl of sliced peach halves, or quarters, whatever, with some cream poured over them. Nothing like simple, and this struck me as a perfect simple dessert, after the chicken and with some coffee.

So we're sitting there with our coffees and desserts, there's a bit of wine left, I cashed a cheque for about $450.00 the other day for some publicity shots, she's got a really neat little fruit flan and I've got my bowl of peaches.

I took a large peach half dripping with 10% cream on my spoon and I said, Sarah, isn't this peach, just by itself, outlined against the dark night, it was dark, it was night, and there were cars of course, I told you, this is Yorkville, you're sitting in these outdoor patios with white tablecloths and black railings or whatever and there is a steady stream of cars, isn't this peach beautiful? And she smiled, she looked embarrassed, maybe she thought it was an off-colour allusion, something like Rupert's comment in *Women in Love* about the fig, and then he tears it open, savage beast savage beast, one of my roommates, Colin, who is quite gay, always says, during that scene, and he proceeds to eat.

In this way, perhaps, Kate Millett was born, ripped prematurely out of her mother's womb at the very idea of a man, even symbolically, wanting to eat, to eat means to consume, and then of course there is all this stuff about the act of eating being aggressive of and by itself, although lovers often bite or nuzzle, kiss and graze with the teeth.

I don't really think her reaction had anything to do with this. I said, No, it really is beautiful, isn't it? And you get real contrast holding it up to the dark but under the light like this.

And Sarah said, You really are a bit of a hippie or something, Doug, sometimes I think you'd be really happy living on a farm somewhere outside of Toronto, complete with your roommates, and maybe some dogs, she added.

So the great and perfect love of our graduation summer was not perfect after all. It was obviously meant to flare up, gestate some real red and blue flame colours, I like that image of Sarah, red lips, blue eyes, and hot all over, silken skin that almost in the summer burns you when you touch it for a second.

It wasn't the punk stuff by itself, it was the combination, I think, of the punk interest, the photography, and my other interests.

I would turn up wearing funny clothes, wildly multicoloured long shorts, running shoes with no socks, magenta sunglasses, t-shirts with exploding black suns and esoteric slogans, that I thought were really neat, and Sarah would say, God, you look bizarre, and then we would sit and talk or have a drink or collapse into bed. But I don't think it was the punk by itself. I think she wanted one of the parts by itself, or, to begin with, she liked me physically quite a bit, and it was summer, and she wanted one of the parts by itself.

All of which is just life, and the summer rolled on, and it was rich with the smell of flowers and bees and stuff like that. We had more good times, moonlit swims, at least 2 or 3, parties, long talks about stuff like family, How do you feel about leaving college, How do I feel, that sort of conversation And I would say, I feel really great about leaving college. No, I never want to go back, cement fortress, isolation discipline, forget it. And she would say, You should accept challenge, you should stay in meds, even though she had laughed at all my doctor jokes when we first met. I went up north and did some wild photographs of the Rebels singing in northern trees, out on northern lakes in rowboats, and so on, and she went to England and saw some plays and went hiking.

But now, after being home for a couple of weeks, and not having seen Sarah since she got back from England, I get Mrs. Carter on the phone. Hello, this is Mrs. Carter. She's in her 50s and she tilts her head back about 4 or 5 inches every time she starts a sentence. It's a nervous thing, neuro, like people who are always playing with their earlobes.

And Mrs. Carter tells me that Sarah is engaged now and they would like me to come to the wedding. I say, O, when is the wedding, next spring? And she says no, no, the wedding is in October, which is cool if you like getting things done in a hurry. I say, That's cool, Mrs. Carter, October is one of my favourite months. The leaves are gorgeous and one of my friends was born in October.

Any way you look at it, it hurts a little bit, like a singing electric wire pulled out of the wall. But any way you look at it I'm going to enjoy going to the wedding. The guy she's engaged to is in meteorology. I know, these stories about the heart, capsizing or flying straight up like a red white & blue helicopter, have always been strange; but as society densifies, and the cities go into grid-lock, then our stories about the heart become even more bizarre. I know this guy slightly. His name's Grant Purnow. We went to Northern Secondary together, and I think I played ping-pong with him once or twice.

If she was engaged to a doctor I could wear a black t-shirt to the wedding with a neat slogan that says something like, Doctors are a medical lobby group. They are as far as I'm concerned. Great healers of broken arms and babies that cough too much. But a weatherologist? Okay. A guy, I guess he's going to lecture on weatherology, or he's going to become a weather analyst, and they'll go camping a lot in the summer, build their own U-hitch trailer and go white-water rafting and stuff like that. I always thought she was more into sitting around and listening to Baez sing "Pity The Poor Immigrant," but of course that's not really where I'm at anyway, as duly noted, okay?

But I am going to enjoy going to the wedding. Sarah phoned herself, naturally, about a week later, and we talked, and it was wonderful, and she said she'd really like me to take pictures, because I'm such a wonderful photographer. But I said, No, no, I don't think so, I think you should get a studio guy, someone who does wedding pictures. I do stuff like a Grateful Dead fan falling out of a tree, or half a dozen meds students with towels and boxer shorts dancing to Jane's Addiction, a tough LA-based group I'm really keen on, or a really nice picture I got of Sinéad O'Connor at a little outdoor restaurant in Toronto called Oblivion way down southwest of the railway tracks in an area of old factory buildings, and she was leaning forward waving away smoke from a guy's cigarette while she was talking to him, heavy-set guy, jowls, smoking Gitanes. It was at night and I got a perfect picture, she didn't mind, of her leaning forward with this wonderful look in her eyes, smoke like evanescent cotton batten, and her mouth open as if really surprised at something being said, No, I'm not sure at what.

BLUE IS A FOCUS OF MEMORY

I MET MARION IN A BOOKSTORE, A BIG PLACE WITH LOTS OF MAG-
azine racks, on Queen Street West, where else? This was when I first
came to Toronto and I used to hang out a lot at some of the clubs
around Queen & Spadina, which used to be the centre of the old
garment district but is now clubs, restaurants, bookstores, and a lot
of young trendy clothing stores, Kimono, Africa, places like that.
That was at least 2 years ago, more probably, I don't want to think
about it. We haven't really gone out together for a year & a ½. I
shouldn't think about it. I have other stuff to think about.

We met in Pages, which is a really good bookstore across from Le
Bistingo, a restaurant none of us could afford to eat in. She was
reading some magazines, copies of *Vogue, Elle,* I don't know what
all. I was glancing at some of the, uh, literary magazines. Not that I
have any pretensions of wanting to be a writer or anything like that,
but I did a number of English courses when I was at college out
west, before coming here to live in the big city, multiculturalism,
millions of people, money floating up and down in the elevators of
60-storey buildings. Anyway our eyes met, I was standing fairly
close to her. I'm here in Toronto to show them, after a while maybe,
what a Manitoba boy can do in regard to business, and of course
I'm interested in meeting people, right? So, our eyes met.

Her's are huge and blue, now that's a cliché, it's also what they
call a received image. But fuck it, some people *do* have large blue
eyes. Marion really does. They're huge and blue. Not huge and blue
and innocent. Her face is innocent, I guess, most girls have innocent
faces when they're nineteen. I'm 26 and I look at least 28. She's 19

and she could be any age from 17 to 30. One of those faces, ineffable, that's a good word, and just a shade common, not that I'm anything special, I guess, beautiful and sort of knowing, with these huge cool faintly speckled blue eyes.

So our eyes meet, and one of us laughs, and we start talking. I ask her if she'd like to go for a beer and she says sure, let's go to the bar at Garbo's, which turns out to be this fairly swank place, normal prices at the bar, and the bar itself in question is a huge long solid dark wood bar from the original Grand Hotel in Brussels where Greta Garbo stayed at least once or twice and perhaps drank at this very bar, and where Sarah Bernhardt used to stay and where she too perhaps leaned forward on her elbows and drank, I don't know what, Belgian beer perhaps or maybe cognac.

This was the beginning of my infatuation, correct word, I think, with Marion. I don't know what love is. I know what sex is. I think infatuation is hard to define but it means you're impressed with the other person, and curious about them, as if they have tricks you're impressed with but you don't quite understand. Pete Wilkins used to pitch for my high school team in Manitoba. He had tricks, he had a pitch that he called the floater, for example, it was like a sneaky pink lady gin drink of a pitch. But I wasn't infatuated with Pete, I just admired him in a way. Anyway.

So we started going out together. And I was shocked after the first or second night by how sexually uninhibited she was. I guess I should have been pleased. Well, I guess I was. But I was also shocked. She did things with total abandon, casualness, and great pleasure, that I had only read about. Innocent guy, what can I say? But I wasn't that innocent, not really. She was extreme. She was hot. She was a scorcher.

And drink? She would get up out of bed, we would be at my apartment over Donaldson's Hardware store on King Street, and stroll as casually as a relaxed sleepwalker over to the kitchen counter area, after an hour or more of all-out fucking and sucking, and stand there at the counter relaxed, leaning forward slightly or raising one graceful white arm to the top cupboard, weight on one angular hip, looking as cool and calm and perfect as a model in a fancy *Vogue* ad, or *Elle,* perhaps, one of those magazines she was reading that day we first met, in Pages, dressed in a loose western shirt unbuttoned to the point where you could see most of one breast, a pair of faded black jeans with pink ankle socks, and a fairly useless print cotton skirt over the jeans. She was beautiful. Sometimes in certain light she would really look, I thought, like one of the great beauties in the history of the world. In bright afternoon sunlight she looked commoner. She had magnificent, write-your-movie-magazine-a-fan-letter eyes. She had an almost perfect body and, strangely, that often seemed one of the lesser sexual aspects about her.

You can probably see this story, or its first main point, coming from a mile away, like a bunch of cattle hoving up in the landscape somewhere west of Winnipeg.

We lasted for about 3 months. It was pretty close to 3 months. She slept around, I think, just about every night we weren't together, and that was quite a few because I was working late until 8 or 9 o'clock Wednesdays, Thursdays, and sometimes Fridays as well. I don't think she even cared that much who she slept with. They were people, I came to realize, that she met on the street, on streetcars, in cafés, sitting outside in the warm weather or sitting inside reading a book, usually a biography of somebody like Edie or some Monaco princess, or bars of course, or clubs. I was working for the Coles book company. They're a franchise. They own dozens of soup-to-nuts bookstores across the country. I started off in the head office, went to the main warehouse for inventory training, I didn't need any, and was then put in charge, significance, of the downtown Yonge store for what turned out to be a long time before I was promoted further.

So our eyes would meet. Those huge yellow-flecked blue eyes, like big flowers of some kind, wild flowers, and she would say, "Oh, nothing, I just hung out for a while with Cora." Or Pat, or Jane, or Serena.

And then she moved in with somebody, a guitarist, by the name of Steve, I'm not sure if he has any other name. But we would still see each other. Nothing to do with borrowing money or anything like that. And not exactly what you would call emotional support. I mean we wouldn't have conversations where she would say, "No, I'm not doing very well," and then I would say, "How can I help." No, it wasn't like that.

I would get off work around 9 o'clock and meet Marion for coffee, a snack, she has acquired strange eating habits, or maybe a drink, at this club or that restaurant, nowhere special, and we would just talk. And she would often seem stronger on me than ever. Sometimes we would go back to my place and fuck. She would get up from the bed and stroll over to the kitchen counter area with that languid walk, reach one slow lazy perfect white arm up to the cupboards and pour herself a big snifter of cognac from the bottle I kept there, 2 or 3 of them actually, mostly because I thought it was classy, like other little things I do to make myself a bit more distinct, less of a cowboy, red braided leather belts, galluses, that's what they call them in Toronto, yellow paisley galluses, in Manitoba we call them braces but in Toronto the big moose call them galluses. She would drink it slowly but without interruption, standing with her back to me, 4, 5 ozs, rolling her lovely blonde head slowly from one side to the other, releasing a short clear gasp of pleasure after the last sip. Then she would come back to the bed, put one knee on the mattress, lean down and say, "It's late, I guess I've really got to go now." And I'd say okay.

There's a whole area of Toronto which I think is committed to the establishment of a world-state stock market backed up by major engineering companies, big hospitals, mining concerns, giant Mies van der Rohe office towers and so on; and there is also a whole area of Toronto which is a sort of neon Rome, committed to the destruction, the scorch and burn of puritanism in their own lives, a sort of casual and graceful surrendering to the moment of pleasure.

I'm working at a respectable job for the moment. I don't know what I'm going to do next. I wear a white shirt and a loose blue smock-type jacket to work every day. I read a bit, I take streetcars, I don't have a car, I listen to 1000s of songs.

Marion wakes up in the morning, which is usually around 2 in the afternoon; a piece of toast slathered with butter & jam, a telephone call, she'll sometimes use a whole tube of shampoo in the course of one shower, a trash magazine, a $10.00 copy of *Vogue,* she just surrenders, glides through, rubs up against, sniffing, turning her head this way or that, strokes her own body, her lithe stomach, rolling her hips against the door frame as she talks to somebody.

I go through a lot of mental reasoning at work. I do klutzy telephone-operator scenes out of Lily Tomlin, just for my amusement, for Paul's or Harry's amusement, I really like her, I think she is really an incredibly talented remarkably brilliant woman, slowing things down, putting in unnecessary gaffes and hooks, the whole bit, one of the secretaries comes back from the washroom and she says, "The washroom's in a real mess."

Whereas Marion just pads across the bare green lino tiles of my apartment over the hardware store on dark King Street above the lake as gracefully as a punk model. She hasn't had an assignment for about a year, except for a couple of underwear ads a few months ago. She's 20. She has a perfect mind, no concepts, but at the same time infinite, blue like the sky, housed simply as an observation point behind a lovely face at the top of a casual body.

I've been reading some of the books at work, *I'm OK, You're OK*, that's an old one, I think, I read that a couple of weeks ago, but yeah, I'd like to shake things up a bit, I don't know what. I'm too restless to sleep all day, you have to have money, even South American wristwatches with funny umbrellas on the face cost money. I go on working, and listening to music, because that's where it's at, but I don't even go to clubs very much in the evening. Marion goes out and comes home late, I'm not always sure where she goes. "O God, I'm not doing a thing with myself." Or, "One of these days, my parents are going to kill me." She likes to illuminate the perfection of her life, even the act of eating a piece of cold pizza out of the fridge at 4 o'clock in the morning for supper by stressing tension with her parents. They're 2nd generation Ukrainian. Hard-working yokels who have made good money, in the restaurant business, and retired to Richmond Hill at the far north edge of Toronto. Lots of room and a well-earned backyard. Who keep waiting for Marion to become a fashion model.

My parents are German and Italian, they have a farm, out in Manitoba, and, apart from the farm, they don't have a great deal of money. I guess they spend it all on the cows.

What may start wearing off, I think, is the self-destructive thing. I was thinking the other day about how much vicarious pleasure I seem to get from Marion's different attitude games of throwing herself down and seeing how beautifully she can get back up. Of course, she gets a cheque from her parents. But I do enjoy the way she flirts with excess. Not that she's started turning up with dark circles under her eyes. She never shoots dope. Maybe that's what I should do, come to think of it. Maybe I should get hooked on white stuff, horse, smack, quit my job, straighten out, and then write a book about music. I'm just a neat guy who failed bass Fender guitar in high school, or something. She snorts a fair bit, not at home, but I know she does with friends when she's out, this club, that club, hangouts.

And she's dependent, in various ways. Cool, but it turns out she's dependent, first one, then the other.

That's what's different about Paul and Harry at work. They don't hang around the clubs that much. But they are cool. And funny. And they're not dependent.

We're just crazy about each other, I guess. So maybe this is cool, or cool for right now. I seem to spend a lot of my time going back and forth to work on the King streetcar, reading magazines, listening to Jane's Addiction on my Sony Walkman, and Parachute Club, and Cowboy Junkies. Cowboy Junkies are a Toronto group. They're different, they're very hot right now.

What she enjoys about me is, I think, the image she has of me coming from Manitoba, clean-cut vibrant young farm stock. O that's me, clean shaven, and I even use a touch of Brylcreem to keep the cow-lick down. She likes that.

She likes to think of herself as beautiful and doomed. I sent out for pizza or Chicken Chalet one night, it was late, we had just made love. She was walking languidly across the green lino tiles of our main room saying something really non-sequiturial about "Tough pickers play from the hip." That's something about us. We both like music terms.

And I said, I was lying on the bed, naked, a cool breeze coming in off the lake or at least off King Street, ½asleep, "You mean young pickers play the blues down low." And she said, That's a nice phrase, yeah, I like that. So I kept it. They play down low and they call it punk, but it is a blues lament kind of sound, like a white dove with its throat cut released in darkness, that turns ice blue before it flies up into the light.

I turn 27 in December. My own concept of punk and the pleasure of flirting with excess, making danger, or death, or simply going over a line and coming back, into a substitute for living by a set of rules, and after all I obviously do live by a set of rules, is more of a cowboy image, an image of somebody who can do these things but not get lost in the pleasure of their own absorption.

But she's beautiful, there's no two ways about that.

Other things are hot right now. I get hot at work sometimes when certain things don't work out right. That isn't a very good sentence, it's not very clear, not clear like some of the pictures in the art gallery I was looking at over the weekend, we went to see a friend do a performance piece, he read a short essay from some almanac, about chickens, with an egg in his mouth while he read. I guess that's trendy. I walked around and looked at the pictures. I have to read more, I'm not going to give up my interest in music, but I have to read more. This is hot.

A certain indefinable scent, the sex is so good I find it difficult to motivate myself in certain directions. It's easier for me if I think about certain things while I'm at work. I keep the Walkman on a large part of the time. I do take-offs on Richard Lewis for the guys in accounting when I go in to check an invoice against our computer inventory.

Marion is probably moving anyway. Who knows? Toronto is traffic city, it's far out. Some of our jokes. She is the only person who takes my ex-philosophy major, for 2 years, heavy comments about Hawaiian influences on the Pixies, Frank Sinatra crossing over and being reborn as David Bowie, Sinéad O'Connor as a strangled choir girl, stuff like that, as opposed to my doing impressions, mugging, things I know I'm good at, seriously. So I would miss that, I think.

I only listen to music away from work for perhaps an hour a day. I almost never read the junk magazines. Ok, I sneak a look. I know I have to read more. It doesn't matter what I want to do, I know I have to be more open to ideas. Sometimes when we're making supper together, she's got black spandex and a short skirt and one of my underwear vests on, some simple thing, putting rice and tomatoes in an oven dish, something like that, our eyes meet, and I start laughing, I'm in a good mood, my eyes are dark and a little strained, I'm always trying to come up with the right move, her eyes are like the ocean.

A NOTE ON THE TEXT

WHAT'S SO EASY ABOUT 17?

This poem came to me very quickly and I can't give you a personal reason as to Why? It's certainly not a glorification of wild driving. I've always loved cars and highways. It's not a tract against wild high school or young 20s drivers. There are no older people, truckers, or families in the poem. I like the various social details that become part of the experience. I think the poem is a metaphor for a variety of other things besides driving. Also I think it's more exciting, in a positive way, than a lot of poems about grandfathers or landscapes and so on. I wrote it very quickly on a hot dusty July morning with my head full of Ontario streets and highways.

THE AMAZINGLY CALM FACE OF THE YOUNG PALESTINIAN BOY

Exoticism is a strange word that turns up and flips around, often quite subjectively, in just about everybody's travel impressions. In a city like the greater Metropolitan Toronto spread, we are all travelling to some degree all the time. As time goes on, it may be debatable as to who becomes seen as exotic.

PEOPLE AT NIGHT

This is a Toronto poem, but it struck me some time after writing it that a lot of the poem has a suggestion of Rome in the late 40s. I don't know how to explain this exactly, it's summer, there are a lot of outdoor cafés, there's a certain rhythm of life, the city is very multicultural, and there is a very strong Italian population that has influenced a number of dynamics including, very slightly, language.

AVA

I don't know why I wrote this poem. It was a gorgeous hot day and I was thinking of Ava Gardner for some reason, and of a club I like a lot that I'd been to recently. I haven't seen a lot of her films, but I think of her as a woman who, compared to Lana Turner, let's say, was a remarkable woman and a really genuine icon.

LOST BUFFALOS

I think "Lost Buffalos" goes beyond comparing Ottawa to Washington. It's a piece of pure continental sociology turned around and presented in emotional literary anecdotes that have their own qualities of language and story, something Chaucer might have liked, for example, as a poem in 4 parts, with a running pattern that involves gender and birthplace and attitude, and is finally, I think, about region and individual sense of place.

ANNOUNCING BAGHDAD

"Announcing Baghdad" is not a poem about the war in the Persian Gulf, it's a poem about some of the media we watched during that period of about 3 months. That's why I start with Madonna, not because I don't like her, but because people praise her for being a rebel, and from Madonna I go on to Schwarzkopf who became something of a media hero after the war. The poem is a bit like a photograph laid over a photograph: the text is not directly about the bottom photograph, it *is* directly about the top photographs, so it's about us. As for moral attitudes, Do I think the war was mismanaged? Yes, I do. Grossly. Women and children, in one of the oldest cultures in the world, were killed in some of the air strikes over Baghdad. What more can I say?

TOBACCO HEAVEN

I call this poem "Tobacco Heaven," aware that the two words are a shade contradictory, because it often seems to me that a lot of southern Ontario has, at times, a sort of groundlessly optimistic view of current events which, in turn, other people, younger layers, come up against and feel confused, disaffected, rebellious.

PHILADELPHIA

I don't think people who rush out to claim architects like Harold Cardenal or Raymond Moriyama as "major Canadian architects" are standing in the way of those architects in regard to larger acclaim, no, they're more of a building block, if I can make a small double entendre. But nevertheless, this "major Canadian" label is a holding pattern. We don't have a concept of trying to sell our major talents to other parts of North America; and if they leave, which they sometimes do, then we feel we've lost them. I go for walks in Toronto and I feel that Frank Lloyd Wright is with me even though he died several generations ago, and I was born in Ontario. Similarly, I would like to walk down a street in New York or Toronto, and see a Harold Cardenal building across the street from a Phillip Johnson building. Once the hype fades, I think the Harold Cardenal building is going to be the most impressive. So Cardenal and Moriyama are geniuses, and we should praise them; but we should also compare them to other people in the North American spectrum.

WHO SAYS JEFF KOONS IS POSTMODERN?

This poem started with a very graphic image of a brown paper bag used as a baffle or a mask, and then developed into reflections on different areas of contemporary pop. The poem is concerned with how simple music can be and still be extremely effective, although I admit tons of garbage gets reproduced by certain groups. This poem touches on personal alienation to some degree and glances at some of the subjects that come up in contemporary pop. I think it's a good poem compared to possibly more "universal" subjects, but it is limited, it starts with the image of the brown paper bag, and it's not intended as a total statement about contemporary pop or punk. As an added note, I don't think that Jane's Addiction are as musically great as Gustav Mahler. On the other hand, I think they're extremely good, and I think they deserve to be talked about.

ACKNOWLEDGEMENTS

Thanks to Sam Solecki, Ellen Seligman, and Linda Williams for helping to push this new boat into the water. I would also like to thank all the bookstores that allow me to browse at will; and several bars and restaurants where I drop in at lunch-time just for coffee, with a friend or a book.

"Clarities" and "Cities" were published in *Poetry Canada Review* some time ago; "Open House" appeared in an almost absolutely different version except for one or perhaps two lines; almost all of the other poems in *China Blues* are from an intensive period covering late spring and summer 1991.

Special thanks to Wendy Furtado at the Alliston Public Library for her comments on Jane's Addiction and the English group The Cure.

Further thanks to The Canada Council and the Ontario Arts Council for their continued support; and to the Ministry of Culture and Communications for their support of the Writer-In-Residence Library Program.